LEE LOCKWOOD

Conversation with Eldridge Cleaver

ALGIERS

JONATHAN CAPE
THIRTY BEDFORD SQUARE LONDON

FIRST PUBLISHED IN GREAT BRITAIN 1971
THIS PAPERBACK EDITION FIRST PUBLISHED 1971
© 1970 BY ELDRIDGE CLEAVER AND LEE LOCKWOOD

JONATHAN CAPE LTD
30 BEDFORD SQUARE, LONDON WC I

ISBN 0 224 00552 9

PRINTED AND BOUND IN GREAT BRITAIN
BY BUTLER & TANNER LTD, LONDON AND FROME

JONATHAN CAPE
PAPERBACK
JCP 80

CONVERSATION WITH
ELDRIDGE CLEAVER

by the same author

SOUL ON ICE

POST-PRISON WRITINGS
AND SPEECHES

I want to express my appreciation to Deborah MacPhail, who transcribed the tapes, helped with the editing, typed the manuscript, and gave unstintingly of her time.

L. L.

I think one continues to go back to prison until he gets his shit together, and then he refuses to go back, you know, and that's something else.

—Eldridge

INTRODUCTION

"The record here is that though the petitioner was arrested and his parole canceled more than two months ago, hearings before the Adult Authority have not even been scheduled. There is nothing to indicate why it was deemed necessary to cancel his parole before his trial on the pending of criminal charges of which he is presumed innocent."

"It has to be stressed that the uncontradicted evidence presented to this Court indicated that the petitioner had been a model parolee. The peril to his parole status stemmed from no failure of personal rehabilitation, but from his undue eloquence in pursuing political goals, goals which were offensive to many of his contemporaries. Not only was there absence of cause for the cancellation of parole, it was the product of a type of pressure unbecoming, to say the least, to the law enforcement paraphernalia of this State."

—California Superior Court Justice Raymond J. Sherwin, in his written opinion on granting a writ of *habeas corpus* to Eldridge Cleaver, June 12, 1968

Today, at the very moment I write these words, two white American astronauts are clambering over the moon, joking and singing as they gather up chunks of the lunar landscape, while at the same moment Eldridge Cleaver, American writer, Black Panther leader and journeyman revolutionary, whose avowed mission is to bring heaven down to earth, is in unhappy political exile in Algiers.

If the one voyage represents the apotheosis of our society's material achievement, the other symbolizes its spiritual failure. For Commander Alan Bean and Brother Eldridge Cleaver, two men as unalike as the uniforms they wear, are both logical end products of the American system. Bean, heroic in his silvery-white space suit and helmet, represents the best that America can accomplish when she harnesses vast portions of her technology and wealth to a single purpose. Cleaver, the anti-hero in his black pants, black leather jacket, black beret and black gun—the Panther uniform—embodies the victim's inevitable response to a society willing to invest billions of dollars in space exploration and bloody war while millions of its citizens continue to be afflicted by hunger, poverty, racism, exploitation and repression.

It is this sense of imbalance and injustice in America, an injustice experienced at first hand and every day, that ultimately impels men like Eldridge Cleaver, who would much rather be doing something else, to become revolutionaries. As Cleaver himself puts it in this interview:

> There is no need for anyone to be talking about a war on poverty in the United States of America. What we need in the United States is a war on the rich ... on the system that allows poverty to exist in the midst of all those riches.

I have said that Cleaver is in political exile from the United States. It is important to stress the phrase *political exile* for two reasons: first, because it is the kind of phrase most Americans, with instinctive chauvinism, automatically associate with other countries whose institutions and traditions are, we imagine, less enlightened than our own; second, because there are still many people who regard Cleaver's sudden departure as merely the desperate act of a convict on the lam. Since the facts surrounding the famous "shootout" with the Oakland police are still largely misunderstood, and since it was this event and its consequences that ultimately led to his exile, I shall recount the story here.

In December 1966 (almost exactly two years before his flight into exile), Cleaver was released from Soledad Prison in California, where he had been serving a sentence of up to fourteen years on a conviction for assault with intent to commit murder. Although as a model prisoner he could have been eligible for parole after two years, he was not released until having served fully nine years of his sentence, and then only through the intervention of prominent intellectuals and legal personalities who had become aware of his literary talents and had campaigned on his behalf.

Cleaver filled his first eighteen months of freedom with a frenzy of activity. He became an editor of *Ramparts* (then in its pre-radical phase as a left-liberal Catholic magazine). He published *Soul on Ice,* a collection of original essays and sketches written in prison that won him a national following. He joined the Black Panther Party. And he got married.

Of all these events, probably the most fateful was his

encounter with the Panthers. His own political development paralleled theirs. At the time Cleaver joined their ranks early in 1967, the Black Panthers for Self-Defense was an embryonic group of Oakland blacks who advocated physical resistance to police repression and "related" openly to guns. By the time of his departure eighteen months later, the Panthers had dropped the qualification "For Self-Defense" in favor of an ideological commitment to socialist revolution and reform and had grown into a national organization with chapters in most American cities that have large black ghettoes. When their founder, the charismatic Huey Newton, who was one of the most formative influences upon Cleaver's political education, was jailed in October 1967, Cleaver of necessity became the Party's chief spokesman. As an occupational hazard, he also became a major object of harassment by the Oakland, California, Police Department, then already engaged in aggressive suppression of the Black Panther Party.

Cleaver's brief taste of freedom ended abruptly in Oakland on the night of April 6, 1968. Both the Oakland police and Eldridge Cleaver have given their versions of what happened, but since Cleaver's account of the incident was later corroborated by a California Superior Court Judge in the only "trial" of the evidence that has yet been held (more about this in a moment), I shall summarize it here.

Late on the night of April sixth, a convoy of three cars containing seven Black Panthers was driving slowly through Oakland en route to the home of a friend. Alone in the lead vehicle were Cleaver and a young Panther called "Little Bobby" Hutton. Cleaver, in what may have been his only "illegal" act of the evening, stopped his car and got out to

relieve himself in the street, the other vehicles pulling in behind to wait. At that moment a squad car of Oakland police,
which apparently had been tailing the convoy with its lights
out, arrived at the scene. A spotlight was beamed on
Cleaver's car, and the amplified command was issued for the
two occupants to come out with their hands up. When
Cleaver, who out of modesty had retreated behind the car's
open door, intending to comply with the order, reached
down to zip up his pants, the skittish police immediately
opened fire.

The Panthers in the convoy scattered and took cover.
Some, who were armed, began returning the withering fire
of the police, who had already radioed for reinforcements.
In the darkness, Cleaver and Hutton hurdled a fence and
eventually wound up in the basement of a residence. Hutton
had a shotgun and began firing back. The police replied with
semi-automatic weapons and tear gas. The latter soon became overpowering, and Cleaver, now wounded in the leg,
yelled out that he and Hutton wished to surrender.

With the firing halted, the two men emerged from the
riddled, smoking basement into the white glare of police
lights with their hands in the air, Cleaver limping and stark
naked to show that he had no weapon, Hutton also unarmed, having tossed out his shotgun first. The police were
all around them. At that point, Hutton apparently made
some kind of movement that evoked a stormy crossfire of
police bullets from close range, killing him almost instantly.
The police later claimed that Hutton had tried to run.
Cleaver insisted that Hutton had been shoved by a police-
man. Whichever story is the correct one, it seems clear that
there is no conceivable move that Hutton could have made,

surrounded as he was, unarmed, blinded and choked by tear gas, that would have justified his execution by the Oakland police.

Eldridge Cleaver, taken first to a hospital and then to jail, was indicted along with the five other living Panthers on charges of assault with intent to kill. His bail, set at $50,000, was quickly raised by friends. Yet still he could not go free. Before daybreak of April seventh, only a few hours after the shootout, members of the California Adult Authority held an extraordinary meeting by telephone and voted to revoke Cleaver's parole. The Adult Authority (which in other states is called the parole board) ordered Cleaver returned to prison on three specific charges of parole violation: (1) possession of a weapon; (2) association with individuals of bad reputation; (3) failure to cooperate with his parole officer.

No one lacking access to all the facts should attempt to pass judgment on the truthfulness of these allegations. However, three comments can be made concerning these charges that seem to throw into question the motives of the Adult Authority:

1. Eldridge Cleaver maintains that he himself had been unarmed, that the only weapon found in the house where he and Hutton had taken refuge was Bobby Hutton's shotgun. However, if Cleaver *had* had a gun (or if he had used Hutton's), then presumably the Adult Authority should have charged him with the much more serious offense of having fired it at the police (assault with intent to kill). Yet they charged him only with the less consequential (and perhaps harder to prove) crime of possession.

2. The "individuals of bad reputation" were simply

Cleaver's fellow Panthers. (At least that is the supposition, since they were not even listed by name in the Adult Authority's charge.) However, as brought out in subsequent testimony, Cleaver had received specific permission from his parole officer to work in the Black Panther Party.

3. The California Adult Authority, the majority of whose members are former police officials, public prosecutors and penal authorities, has dictatorial powers over parole matters and can rescind a convict's parole instantaneously on a quorum vote. One member, acting alone, can suspend a parole indefinitely. If Cleaver had, as was charged, failed to cooperate with his parole officer, then it seems highly unlikely—given the number of influential enemies he had made in the state government from Governor Reagan down —that the Adult Authority would have waited until a shooting incident before canceling Cleaver's parole.

It may be that the Adult Authority is so accustomed to having its way in such matters that it did not bother to make its charges legally consistent. If so, great indeed must have been its shock two months later, when California Superior Court Judge Raymond J. Sherwin, after hearing an application by Cleaver's attorneys for a writ of *habeas corpus,* ordered him released from prison and his parole status restored. Judge Sherwin, exhibiting a remarkable disinclination to toe the political line (and a unique disinterest in his own professional future), delivered a written opinion that is a model of judicial candor. It made two basic points: (1) The Attorney General's Office of the State of California, which presented the evidence on behalf of the Adult Authority, had failed utterly to substantiate any of the charges against Cleaver; (2) It was clear that Cleaver was "a model parolee," and that the real reason his parole had been canceled was because of his political activities— "a type of pressure unbecoming, to say the least, to the law enforcement paraphernalia of this State," in Judge Sherwin's words.*

So Cleaver was at liberty once more, but again his freedom was to be short-lived, for the Adult Authority immediately went to the State Appellate Court and succeeded in obtaining a reversal of Judge Sherwin's decision. Significantly, this reversal was granted on a technicality. The Appellate Court did not hold that Judge Sherwin's evaluation of the evidence was wrong; it merely affirmed that his court had no authority to hear the case in the first place because, according to the statutes of the State of California, the Adult Authority has absolute jurisdiction in determining cases of parole violation in that state. In other words, what the Appellate Court, and later the State Supreme Court, which upheld it, maintained in effect was that if you are a parolee, the Adult Authority may at any time revoke your parole by accusing you of anything it wishes, and you do not have the right to a fair trial of the evidence on which the charges are based.

November 27, 1968, was therefore set as the date when Cleaver was ordered to report back to prison. It has probably occurred to some readers that Cleaver's lawyers could have instituted a suit against the State of California on the grounds that Cleaver's constitutional rights were being infringed upon by the Adult Authority. True, but such constitutional cases take years to fight through the courts. Mean-

* Judge Sherwin's Excerpts from opinion appear at the beginning of this Introduction.

while, Eldridge Cleaver would have remained in jail, and it is not impossible that he might have served the full five remaining years of his term before the suit reached the Supreme Court.* When, a few days before the November twenty-seventh deadline, U.S. Supreme Court Justice Thurgood Marshall (a Negro) refused to grant a stay of the order, Cleaver, having exhausted his legal appeals and having vowed never again to return to prison, dropped quietly from sight.

I I

Though I had long admired his book, *Soul on Ice,* and though we had friends in common, I met Eldridge Cleaver for the first time in Cuba. In America, we lived on opposite coasts and belonged, really, to different worlds. Cuba is a wonderful place for reconciling such differences. In that hothouse of revolution and charged hope, all kinds of people meet and form relationships that would be unlikely to occur almost anywhere else in the world.

I arrived in Havana in early May 1969, on a journalistic

* Still, Cleaver, who is famous and has the support of excellent lawyers, might have had a chance. There must be many other men in a similar predicament who cannot afford or attract the legal aid necessary to fight such a case. It is small wonder that so many men who go to prison for the first time fail to rehabilitate themselves upon their release, when it is made so clear to them that as parolees they are second-class citizens who have no rights. For a black ex-convict, such an experience must be doubly degrading and alienating. For thousands of them, traditionally, there has been but one place for them to go: back to jail. Recently, for many, there has been another: the Black Panther Party.

mission of quite another sort. Friends met me at the airport, and as we were riding into town one of them, a Cuban, asked me if I would like to meet Eldridge Cleaver. It was then more than five months since he had disappeared from the United States. I was surprised, not so much at the news that he was there—though he had been rumored to be living in such disparate places as Canada, Sweden, North Vietnam and various African nations, Cuba had always seemed to me the logical place for him to be—as at the apparent openness of the secret, since as yet there had been nothing published in the U.S. press concerning his whereabouts. I told my friend that I would indeed like to meet him, and she promised to arrange it. The next day, he called me at my hotel.

"Hello, this is Eldridge."

"Eldridge! How do you do. I'm glad to hear your voice," I said. (What else does one say in such a situation?) "How are you?" His reply sounded surprisingly dispirited:

"Well . . . just hangin' on—you know?"

I invited him to dinner the following evening. He accepted, but he expressed concern about eating in a public place where he might be spotted by a Western newsman or diplomat. I suggested that we dine in my hotel room, pointing out that it would be both safer and also more convenient, since at that time all the restaurants in Havana, including those in the hotels, were packed full from the moment they opened until well after midnight when the food ran out, and it was usually necessary to wait in line for a table from one to four hours. Hotel room service also required great patience, but at least in one's room one could wait in comfort.

I had offered to arrange to have a car pick him up, but he had said that he lived only a few blocks away and preferred to walk over. At about six-thirty the next evening, I went out of the Alhambralike Hotel Nacional and down the length of its long formal driveway, thinking to wait for him at the corner and thus cut down the time he would have to be walking alone. Twenty-first Street, a busy thoroughfare which feeds downhill directly into the Hotel Nacional's driveway, was crowded with Cubans of all skin hues returning home from work or lined up waiting for buses or restaurant tables or simply standing around in groups in the middle of the sidewalks, conversing animatedly.

In the midst of this genial hubbub, I picked out Eldridge clearly a block away. He was a head taller than all the Cubans in sight and dressed in sandals without socks (in Cuba, sandals are worn barefoot only by women, homosexuals and foreigners), baby-blue jeans, and a pink gaucho shirt which the late afternoon sun lit up as startlingly as if it had been dyed in Day-Glo paint. He moved down the opposite sidewalk at a leisurely pace halfway between a stroll and a prowl, his powerful shoulders erect, his head thrust forward a bit, his eyes invisible behind dark green shades. His black Oriental beard, which, according to rumor, he had shaved off when leaving the United States, seemed fully restored. I watched with trepidation as he ambled slowly past the office of the Associated Press, which is located on the ground floor facing the street and at that hour always has it doors and windows open wide. ("I didn't know that AP *had* an office in Havana," he said later.) At the corner, he caught my signal and began crossing over toward me. As he drew closer, I noticed that he seemed surprisingly fleshy around the middle, an observation that vaguely troubled me though I don't know why, unless for the implication it carried that Eldridge Cleaver might be going to seed in Cuba.

He was noticeably ill at ease in the lobby of the hotel, but once upstairs in my room he relaxed, dumping himself into a chair and appreciatively lighting up one of my Kents while I got on the phone and went through the laborious ritual of getting first the operator and then room service to answer. Having ordered up as sumptuous a dinner as the kitchen was able to provide, I got two glasses from the bathroom and offered Eldridge a drink of Scotch from a bottle I had brought with me.

For a moment he said nothing. He had taken off his glasses, but his eyes were so nearly closed that he seemed to be either asleep or off in a world of his own thoughts. I wasn't even sure he had heard me. Then, very slowly, he held up his right palm in a gesture of gentle protest, moving it in a little arc in front of him. When he finally spoke it was in a muted voice so soft that he might have been talking to himself in a dream.

"Scotch? . . . Man—I don't know if I can handle Scotch just now, you know?" His hooded eyes opened just wide enough to look at me. "It's been a long time, you know?" The lids hung open an instant longer, then dropped heavily, as if their weight were too much to support. Was he thinking it over? I wondered. At last he spoke again, this time in the firm voice tone of a man who has arrived at a decision:

"All right, why not? Sure, I'll have a drink. Give me some Scotch!"

It suddenly came to me that he was suspicious of me (as well he ought to have been, in his predicament, wary of any American), but that he had decided to trust me at least that much. And so, with the ice thus partly broken, we drank and ate and smoked (the best cigars in the world, of course) and talked our way through the tropical evening, two men of identical nationality but of antipodal origins who, traveling in separate orbits, had accidentally rendezvoused at a point as culturally distant from home as the far side of the moon.

I remember thinking to myself that night that when you sit down to dinner with Eldridge Cleaver, you know you are sitting with a black man. He *is black,* and he makes you think about it; in fact, he never lets you forget it. He is black and you are white. This understanding was communicated with neither hostility nor arrogance, simply in the spirit of recognition—a fact that had to be accepted before a relationship was possible. Though I found this a little disconcerting at first—when you are drawn to someone, you are naturally eager to emphasize the things you have in common rather than your differences—nevertheless, I think I ultimately felt more at ease with Cleaver because of this implicit confrontation.

I was also surprised to learn, as I grew to know him better, that the reserve I had sensed in him at the beginning was not, as I had supposed, merely strategic. It was partly that, but beyond tactics lay the reticence of a naturally shy person, an elementally human quality that I found touching then and even more so later when I reread some of his more aggressive published rhetoric.

At the same time, he projected, beneath the mild exterior, a feeling of great strength—but strength under hair-trigger tension. He was enormously moody. At times he seemed like a man pursued and harried by demons visible only to himself. He had buried alive within him great reserves of anger, ready to explode on slight provocation. I found him one of the most complex and tormented men I have ever met. He seemed to hold within his mind a vast oscillating field of contradictory impulses. These were mirrored in his behavior: alternately he would be shrewd and naïve, tough-minded and soft-hearted, indolent and dynamic, thoughtful and impulsive, indecisive and determined, idealistic and cynical, self-confident and unsure. I do not know how much of this torment was caused by the circumstances in which he found himself, but I suspect they were a considerable factor, for, as I shall explain in a moment, he was under enormous pressure in Cuba. Whatever the case, Cleaver "went through a lot of changes," as he himself often remarked with characteristic candor. Even on first meeting he fearlessly exposed all the facets of his character, rough and smooth, with no apologies. I think it was this quality of existential toughness in Cleaver that impressed me most.

By now it is no secret that something went badly sour between Eldridge and the Cubans. Unfortunately, when our interview took place in Algiers some weeks later, legal considerations prevented us from discussing this subject or even mentioning that Cleaver had been in Cuba at all. What I am setting down here are the things that Cleaver told me in Havana and in subsequent private conversations, as I remember them. Ultimately, of course, it is his experience, and his story to tell in full.* The Cubans' side to this story—which I do not presume to know—may never be told.

In the first place, Cleaver told me, he had chosen Cuba for his place of exile out of admiration for Fidel Castro, Che Guevara and the Cuban people, and also because the Cubans firmly supported other revolutionary movements throughout the world, particularly the black liberation movement in the United States. Sixteen months earlier, at the OLAS Congress of Latin American revolutionaries in Havana, Fidel Castro had publicly embraced Stokely Carmichael and later, in his keynote speech, pledged Carmichael and his fellow black power advocates Cuba's full backing. Cleaver, interpreting this commitment literally, had arrived in Havana expecting to function openly as a recognized black leader. He had hoped to open up a Black Panther Party information office there and to establish liaison between the Party and the many other revolutionary movements that have representation in Cuba. But since Carmichael's visit, Che Guevara had been killed in Bolivia, and the OLAS program had been temporarily shelved by Castro in favor of an all-out domestic effort to right Cuba's dangerously listing economy by producing ten million tons of sugar in 1970. This gigantic effort has required the full attention and participation of all Cubans. Being thus embattled, and thus perhaps unwilling to stir up fresh provocations of the United States, Cleaver's Cuban hosts had made it clear that he was a welcome guest as long as he chose to remain,

* Perhaps he is already writing it as part of his new book—the sequel to *Soul on Ice*—which he is preparing for McGraw-Hill.

but that he must keep his presence quiet and refrain from overt political activity for the time being. For an activist like Cleaver, this was a condition even more confining than the prison term he had fled.

Shortly after his arrival, Cleaver had been taken on a guided tour of the island, visiting most of the showplaces of the Revolution. Once having settled in Havana, however, being without a car and lacking fluency in Spanish, he had been kept in virtual isolation in his apartment. In five months, he had been unable to meet Fidel Castro or any other high Cuban official, except for the Chief of Cuban Intelligence, with whom he had had a brief but angry personal encounter which had only fueled his rising distrust and disaffection. He had also grown suspicious of lower-echelon Cuban officials assigned to work with him, who he felt were not always honest with him. He was almost completely out of touch with his wife, who had remained in San Francisco, and with the leadership of the Black Panther Party. For obvious reasons, he could not speak with them by telephone, and the transmission of mail and messages was slow and sporadic. He suspected—I believe unjustly—that the Cubans were intentionally holding up his communications.

One of his sorest complaints was that his wife Kathleen had not yet arrived in Cuba. According to Eldridge, the Cubans had promised to arrange for her to join him in time to have her baby in Havana. Now she was eight months pregnant, the time was approaching when she would no longer be able to travel, and he had been told that she was having legal difficulties in leaving the United States. Cleaver felt that this was just a lame excuse, that there must be other reasons.

Another source of Cleaver's disaffection was ideological. Cuban revolutionary propaganda has long proclaimed that socialism has eradicated all vestiges of the racial discrimination that was the legacy of the former capitalist society. Cleaver had become friendly with some *negro* musicians and dancers and from them had learned what many white Cubans privately acknowledge, that certain racist attitudes and policies do still remain in spite of efforts to dislodge them. In general, he found that blacks were underrepresented in the upper echelons of leadership and administration, suffered a certain amount of discrimination in job advancement, and were restrained from expressing their "black identity" in such ways as by wearing "Afro" hairdos and clothing and by practicing traditional African religions. From this Eldridge concluded that Cuba's leaders, in giving public support to the black liberation struggle abroad while failing to complete that aspect of their revolution at home, were guilty of a certain hypocrisy.

There were numerous other problems, but the one that ultimately proved to be the most antagonizing, both to Cleaver and to the Cubans, was his association with several of the black highjackers who had sought refuge in Cuba.

When the current rash of highjackings began, about two years ago, the Cubans made an effort to evaluate each case according to what they considered its merits. Those highjackers who came genuinely seeking political asylum, especially if they were black, were usually granted freedom and given a new life. The rest were put in jail or mental hospitals or else were deported. However, as the frequency of incidents rapidly increased, the Cubans, wishing both to avoid international complications and to rid themselves of the logistical headache entailed, changed their policy in order to discourage further highjackings. All highjackers were placed immediately in prison for a period of observation and interrogation. Later on, those who did not appear to be potential criminals were sent to an agricultural work camp in Camagüey Province, some 500 miles from Havana, for an indefinite period of time. In this camp the hours are long, the work is hard, and there are few enjoyments. It is a tough life.

Cleaver had become friendly with several of the first black highjackers, who were living at large in Havana. One of them had married a Cuban girl; another had come with his wife and was living in the Havana Libre Hotel. These and others were eventually recruited by Cleaver into what became, in effect, the Havana chapter of the Black Panther Party. Apparently this alarmed the Cuban officials responsible for Cleaver, although they reluctantly went along with it.

Then occurred an event that brought their relations close to rupture. By coincidence, there had arrived in the Camagüey work camp a black highjacker who had once served time with Cleaver in Soledad Prison in California. In fact, he had still been in jail in California when he heard a rumor that Cleaver was in Cuba. He thereupon made plans to escape from prison and join his old friend. According to Eldridge, this man was able to carry out his plans with such ingenuity that in the space of less than forty-eight hours he had broken out of jail, highjacked an airliner to Havana and landed in another prison—this time a Cuban one!

In due course, the Cubans had sent him to work in the

fields in Camagüey. There, he learned through the underground grapevine the exact location of Cleaver's house. Again he escaped, this time with a companion, and made his way to Havana; there Cleaver welcomed them and gave them "asylum" in his apartment. When the Cuban security police arrived, insisting that the two men must return to the work camp, Cleaver refused to give them up, claiming that they had been mistreated by camp authorities. Furthermore, he bitterly criticized the Cubans for refusing to grant political asylum to highjackers like his friend, who was also an escaped convict and therefore one of the black oppressed of the United States.

One day, I went to visit Cleaver in the *"casa de las panteras,"* as the Cubans called it. It was a penthouse apartment in a residential building on L Street, about halfway between the Havana Libre Hotel (née Hilton) and the sea. Eldridge's apartment, access to which could be gained only by means of a hidden elevator located at the rear of the basement garage, was of commodious size and, except for its lack of air conditioning, quite comfortable. It had an enormous living room, amply and informally furnished, which opened onto a long balcony with an excellent view. Up three steps from the living room was a large dining room and beyond it a spacious kitchen. In Eldridge's bedroom was displayed a giant poster of Huey Newton seated on a wicker throne. On the same wall and also along the hallways hung a number of photographs of Eldridge, taken in various poses and places in the United States, as well as a few of Kathleen. I assume that the apartment possessed several other bedrooms, though I didn't see them, nor did I meet the woman who cleaned up and cooked the Panthers' meals. Several of Cleaver's friends were in attendance, however, lounging on chairs and chaises and quietly digging the blues sounds emanating from an expensive-looking stereo system. It seemed a pleasant place to spend one's exile—if one had to be in exile.

A few days after I met him, Cleaver received a piece of news from the Cubans that temporarily brightened his spirits: his wife was at last on her way to Havana. Then, two days later, something happened that was to have a decisive affect on his status in Cuba. The local correspondent of the Reuters News Agency, acting on a vengeful tip from a mentally disturbed young American lady of Cleaver's acquaintance who had conjured up the unfortunate delusion that he had tried to rape her (spurred, perhaps, by something she had read in *Soul on Ice*), found his way to Cleaver's apartment and transmitted a report that Eldridge Cleaver was living in Cuba. The story was featured on the front pages of American newspapers. Although substantial parts were in error, it contained enough factual truth to throw the Cubans into consternation and make them suspect—though Cleaver claims it is untrue—that he had collaborated with the Reuters correspondent.

A few days later, on the morning of my departure from Cuba, Cleaver called to say he was coming over to tell me something important. He appeared a little later looking visibly agitated. We went for a walk through the hotel's grounds, overlooking the decapitated memorial to the battleship USS *Maine* and the Caribbean. Somewhere ahead, through the sun and mist, was Florida.

"Listen, they're sending me to Algiers," he said as soon as we were alone.

His voice was grim with suppressed anger. The Cubans were upset over the publicity that was being given his presence in Cuba, he said. They wanted him to fly to Algeria on the next plane, which was leaving in two days' time, in order to "take the heat off Cuba," in Cleaver's words. He would hold a press conference in Algiers, stay there for a while, and later on he would be allowed to return quietly to Havana.

He did not believe the latter commitment. Although he wanted to return to Cuba, he said, he was now too suspicious to be able to count on it. As far as he was concerned, he was being given a one-way ticket out of Cuba. His main concern of the moment was to get word to his wife Kathleen and, through her, to the Party. Knowing that I was flying directly to Paris (via Madrid), he asked me to find her and head her off, lest she arrive in Cuba and not find him there. He had no idea where she was, only that she had already left San Francisco. If I found her, I was to tell her to go to Algiers and wait for him there.

It took me half a day to get to Paris and another twenty-four hours to locate Kathleen. My phone calls followed her trail, from San Francisco to New York to, of all places, Paris. After considerable effort, I found out the name of her hotel and arrived there in person only an hour before she was to leave for Orly Airport to take a plane for Algiers, en route to Cuba. She came in very late, breathless, tall and beautifully pregnant, accompanied by Richard Wright's daughter Julia and Emory Douglass, an amiable Panther who was traveling with her as a bodyguard. All three were laden down with shopping bags and bundles. I introduced myself, explaining that I had a message from her husband which I had to deliver in private, and suggested that we go for a walk. Although I might have been an FBI agent for all she knew, she agreed without hesitation, and the others were dispatched upstairs to begin packing while we went outside for a stroll around the corner.

III

Except for the change of scenery, I was surprised to find that Cleaver's situation in Algeria was little different from that in Cuba when I arrived there two weeks later, near the end of June, to interview him. Physically, in fact, it was somewhat worse. The Victoria Hotel, where the Cleavers were staying, will never be listed in any tourist's guide to the city—unless as a hotel to be strictly avoided. Located on a narrow side street in what once was the Arab Quarter, just off the Rue de la Liberté, one of downtown Algiers' busiest thoroughfares, and only a few blocks from the quays of her hyperactive port, it is primarily a hostel for merchant sailors and itinerant small traders. The three stars and the slogan *Dernier Confort* that emblazon the elliptical plaque over its door promise a luxury that is merely relative: it is much better than sleeping on the sidewalks under the arcades as some Arabs still do in that area of the city.

The Cleavers were installed in a small room on the fourth floor of this sleazy establishment in the most uncomfortable circumstances imaginable. Most of the room was filled by the twin beds, which jutted out from the wall almost to the windows. Crowded into the remaining space were a dilapidated armoire packed to overflowing with clothes and with garments also hanging on its doors, a number of trunks and suitcases, and several small tables and chairs, through all of which one had to pick his way to get to the other side of the room. In a corner, behind a shabby curtain, there was a shower, but the toilet was outside in the hall. Every available inch of surface was covered with something: not only a melange of books, magazines, more clothing, and Kathleen's cosmetics, but also such equipment as a large stereo phonograph, an expensive tape recorder, and a combined radio-and-cassette-recorder—all apparently recent acquisitions.

Kathleen, nearing her accouchement, was suffering from a combination of physical exhaustion and nervous tension and was confined to her bed most of the time. There being no restaurant or kitchen in the hotel, Eldridge ate all of his meals outside and brought back food for his wife in a stack of interlocking aluminum lunch pails he had bought in a sporting-goods store in town. Since they were on their own and not the guests of the government, they were running short of money. In addition, there was great uncertainty about where Kathleen would have her baby, now due in a matter of only weeks.

Particularly unsettling to Cleaver was the fact that his status in Algeria was even more in doubt than it had been in Cuba. He had arrived in secret and, contrary to his expectations, the Algerians had not yet granted him permission to publicize his presence. In fact, his entry permit had expired, and he had been unable to see a single government official for a clarification of his status. There was serious question as to whether he would be permitted to remain in the country even clandestinely. Until this problem could be resolved, he was obliged to stay under cover, especially out of sight of the many American tourists and businessmen who thronged the city, and simply wait. (Because of the possibility of an assassination attempt—a fear not so far-fetched in the light of so many unexplained police killings of Panther leaders in the United States—Cleaver usually did not venture into the street without a pistol underneath his jacket or the colorful *dashiki* he often wore.)

In addition, there was the nearly constant pressure from the thousand little crises that beset Eldridge and Kathleen, like any other newly-arrived American couple, in simply coping with living in Algiers. One day, for example, it was decided that Emory Douglass should return temporarily to the United States. Having said his farewells, he went off to the airport in a taxi with Kathleen, while Eldridge and I stayed behind and worked. In due course, Kathleen returned, saying Emory had taken off for Paris. About two hours later, however, the phone rang in the Cleavers' room. It was Emory, calling from Oran. He had gotten on the wrong plane. Now he had to be brought back to Algiers, and then sent off again to Paris. The logistics of solving that one problem occupied an entire day.

It was in the midst of pressure and confusion, after several postponements and with many distractions, that we finally conducted our interview. It took place during the last days of June 1969. There were four sessions of varying lengths held on three different days, each day in a different location. The conversation, which was tape-recorded, ran to more than five hours. The tapes were transcribed in the United States and the transcriptions edited by myself into a version that comprised somewhat more than one-half the original. This was then sent to Eldridge Cleaver in Algiers, who approved it without changes except for the correction of one or two misspellings and wrong dates. Subsequently, Cleaver's attorneys found it necessary to excise about seven pages of the manuscript for legal reasons. It is this slightly adumbrated version that appears here.

It should be clear from this interview that Eldridge Cleaver, though temporarily removed from the American scene, has no intention of "dropping out of history." The subjects discussed are primarily political themes. The *leit-motiv* of the entire conversation is revolution, its theory and its practice. Specifically, it is about the *American* revolution, why it should be made and how it will be made, and the role that Cleaver intends to play in making it. Cleaver has clearly profited from the opportunity forced upon him by his exile to read and reflect about a variety of political subjects. More ideologist than intellectual, he is not only studying and thinking, but laying plans.

The fact that Eldridge Cleaver in exile has become a committed Marxist-Leninist will perhaps astonish no one. What is surprising, and I think more interesting, is that the same process which has radicalized him ideologically has also made him feel, in spite of his circumstances, more of an American. His evaluation of American society is one of the most interesting passages of the interview. In Cleaver's view, what is wrong with America is not its traditional values but the way in which these values have been distorted. As devoutly as any right-wing patriot, he admires the American Constitution and believes in the American Dream. He is a socialist, yet he criticizes all existing socialist governments uniformly for their suppression of individual human liberties. At the same time, he is convinced that socialism will succeed in the United States where it has failed elsewhere because the American people possess "such a strong tradition of democracy" that they would never "stand" for a system that infringed on their civil liberties.

If this is not precisely heresy, it is certainly heterodoxy, and much more in the tradition of Emerson, Whitman and Thoreau than that of Marx, Lenin, Mao and Che. Such a transcendental overview seems all the more remarkable coming from the mind of a black man who has spent most of his life in American prisons and whose own constitutional rights have consistently been denied him by the very society in which he places his unwavering faith.

"What this country needs is a Yankee-Doodle-Dandy form of socialism," says Cleaver. First, however, there must come a violent revolution that will explode the fabric of American society. This revolution will be spearheaded by bloody urban guerrilla warfare. In fact, Cleaver insists, this war has already begun. It is intensifying steadily, as the forces of reaction escalate their repression. By 1972, there will be a right-wing *coup d'état* in this country; this definitive act in turn will trigger the final, all-out conflict which will bring the revolution to power. It is an uncompromisingly grim vision indeed: in order to have Utopia, we must suffer Armageddon first.

I think I should stop interpreting Cleaver and let him speak with his own voice. Concerning the interview, I only wish to add one technical comment about the function of the interviewer. Although the publisher calls this book *Conversation with Eldridge Cleaver,* the title is not quite accurate. "Conversation" implies an equal exchange of ideas between two or more people—a dialectical give-and-take—whereas a good interview, as I see it, is an intentionally unequal dialogue in which the interviewer to a large extent subordinates his own ideas and opinions to the goal of eliciting those of his subject. An interview is neither a conversation nor a debate. It is an inquiry into the state of a person's mind at a finite moment in time.

I could not end this Introduction without saying something about the nationwide repression of the Black Panther Party that is under way in this country today. It is now clear that the legal railroading that forced Eldridge Cleaver into exile was one of the earlier events in the systematic attempt by America's law-enforcement agencies to pick off the Panthers' leaders by either killing them or jailing them on trumped-up charges with excessive bails, and thereby to destroy the Party. It is naïve to assume that the numerous pre-dawn police raids on Panther headquarters across the country—raids that have resulted in numerous slayings and injuries—are not connected to each other and to a central source in Washington. Most of these repressive acts have occurred since the present administration took office. Since then, Vice President Agnew has called the Panthers "a completely irresponsible, anarchistic group of criminals," and both Attorney General Mitchell and J. Edgar Hoover have labeled them "the greatest threat to national security." Jerris Leonard, an Assistant U.S. Attorney General in charge of civil rights, has stated, "The Black Panthers are nothing but hoodlums, and we've got to get them."

The sad truth is that civil liberties and constitutional guarantees are largely a myth in this country in A.D. 1970. Anyone who has ever stood in a police station in a large city watching prisoners being booked will know what I mean. And the situation is growing steadily worse. In a tragic distortion of the spirit of the Bill of Rights, the statutes originally written for the purpose of protecting individual rights are often applied by our so-called law-enforcement agencies in such a way as to deny many people their rights, while other laws are often simply ignored by the very agencies charged with enforcing them. Just as Eldridge Cleaver is in political exile, the Panthers are being murdered for their politics, and nobody is doing very much about it.

One final anecdote to illustrate what the application of American justice can be like if you happen to be Eldridge Cleaver:

Last May, when the Reuters report appeared in American newspapers that Cleaver was in Cuba, the U.S. government decided to cut off his flow of funds. Both of his books were selling well and accumulating considerable royalties with his agent. However, under the "Trading with the Enemy Act," our government can interdict all trade between the United States and certain "restricted" countries, among them Cuba. The "Cuban Assets Control" specifically forbids transaction between U.S. citizens and "Cuban nationals" unless sanctioned by a special Treasury Department license, with the threat of stiff penalties for offenders.

Who is a "Cuban national"? Any citizen of Cuba, would seem to be the logical answer. But that is not all. There exists a little-known Treasury Department regulation under which *Americans* may also be designated Cuban nationals! Even more incredibly, according to this regulation any American who has ever gone to Cuba since July 1963 is eligible for such distinction.*

In due course, Cleaver's publishers and agents were notified that he was now a "designated Cuban national," and that not so much as a dollar was to leave his accounts until his status changed (if ever). Now, aside from the important constitutional question as to whether one's American citizenship is an inalienable right or merely a privilege so fragile that it can be revoked unilaterally by an agency of the federal government, there is also the question of evidence. The Treasury Department's only proof that Cleaver had ever been in Cuba was a Reuters News Agency report—and journalists have been wrong before. However, according to the aforementioned regulation the Treasury Department had merely to *say* that he was a Cuban national, and it was then up to Cleaver and his attorneys to prove that he was *not*.

This travesty of justice endured for four months. Not

* U.S. Treasury Department, Cuban Assets Control, Regulations and Related Documents, July 8, 1963, Paragraphs 515.301, 515.302 and 515.305.

until the middle of September—by which time Cleaver had been living publicly in Algiers for three months—were his lawyers successful in obtaining a rescision of the order. It came in a form fittingly Kafkaesque, a Treasury Department License with its attendant bureaucratic jargon, addressed to Mr. Eldridge Cleaver, San Francisco, California:

Sirs:

1. Pursuant to your application of September 1, 1969, the following transaction is hereby licensed:

YOU MAY BE REGARDED AS A PERSON WHO IS NOT A DESIGNATED NATIONAL OF CUBA.

The Treasury Department rectified its "error," but it didn't phrase it strongly enough. Eldridge Cleaver, journeyman revolutionary, has an American soul which no regulation can alter. He has lived in Castro's Cuba, and now he is in Algiers, the home of Fanon, who "legitimized the revolutionary impulse to violence" of the black man against his white oppressor. One day soon, if we are to believe his sworn promise, he will be coming home to fight and die in the American revolution.

INTERVIEW

I

LOCKWOOD. Eldridge—

CLEAVER. I was going to say, don't call me Eldridge. I forgot; I was thinking of something else.

LOCKWOOD. That's your name—isn't it? Eldridge Cleaver?

CLEAVER. Well, I've been using other names. I once forgot my name at a certain point when it was crucial. I was confronted by an official—a hostile official—and he said, "What's your name? . . . I couldn't think of it.

LOCKWOOD. Tell me what's happened to you during the last eight months of your life.

CLEAVER. You're talking about since November? Well, since November I've traveled extensively throughout the world. I've seen many people under many skies. I've had ups and downs; I've been happy and I've been uptight. I guess you could say that I've continued to experience situations that have exercised the full range of my emotions: from being extremely uptight to complete ecstasy. And that's the truth.

LOCKWOOD. Are you in exile now?

CLEAVER. Am I in exile? Well, I don't really know what the definition of that word is. If it means that I am outside of the borders of the land of my birth, really against my will but out of perceived necessity from political persecution, then I would say yes, I am in exile. People are sometimes referred to as political exiles; I think I would fall somewhere in that category.

LOCKWOOD. Would you say that you are in voluntary political exile?

CLEAVER. Well, when you are deported by the government of your country, I guess that would be *in*voluntary exile. I was not deported. I ran away—a fugitive—in order to elude being sent to prison. So to that extent it was voluntary. I volunteered not to go to the penitentiary.

LOCKWOOD. When did you make that decision?

CLEAVER. The specific decision had to do with the aftermath of the shootout in Oakland on April sixth of last year . . . 1968. But really, my basic decision had to do with my experience in prison when I stayed there for that long stretch. I had decided to change my life and to never return to prison. That was my basic desire, and I've never changed it. So when I found myself in that situation again as a result of that April sixth incident—you know that I was in jail at Vacaville for sixty days—I made up my mind that if I couldn't get out through a writ of *habeas corpus* filed by my attorney, then I had no intention of remaining in prison.

Because I thought that it was very clear to a large majority of the people who were watching and who were interested in the case that justice was on our side, I felt it was necessary to just flatly defy this court order.

LOCKWOOD. And what would you have done if you had escaped from prison—gone underground?

CLEAVER. It was always a question of either going underground in the United States or leaving the United States. I could not have escaped and then walked the streets.

LOCKWOOD. But if you had stayed in this country and gone underground, wasn't there a very good chance that you would have been hunted down by the police and perhaps killed?

CLEAVER. Yes. But you see, we all believe in what Bakunin and Nachaev said in the very first statement of the *Catechism of a Revolutionary:* that a revolutionary is a doomed man. That is, if you're not able to come to terms with the prospects of death, then you have no business at all in defying or confronting or even arguing with the power structure. As a matter of fact, given the climate that has developed in the United States, you don't have any business marching on a picket line if you're not willing to put your life on the line. You don't have any business even attending a convention of the Democratic Party if you're not willing to risk your life. You don't have any business even being in the Bay Area, or any other area of the United States, if you're not willing to risk your life.

We used to keep a record, like a scoreboard, of the number of people being killed by the police all over the country. And you would be surprised that hardly a day goes by that you don't have to add another notch to that board. So you come to terms with the idea that you may be killed. Long before my parole situation came to a head, I had accepted the fact that I might be killed at any moment. The first time in my life that I had to deal with that was when I went to prison. In prison, people are killed or stabbed to death without warning. And when you have to live with the prospect of being wiped out in a flash, you either stop doing what you're doing and remove yourself from that situation, or else you have to accept it and kind of repress it, and get it off your mind. Otherwise, you'll be nonfunctional. You can't walk around afraid and watching and looking over your shoulder. Anyway, I think many people these days have learned to live with that understanding. I learned to live with it somehow.

LOCKWOOD. Do you consider yourself a "doomed man"?

CLEAVER. Well I'm optimistic, you know, and I'm hopeful. But I have no illusions about what my future might be, simply because I know what my future plans are. The more I think about my future plans, the more I consider the possibility that my life will not be very long. I have some rather ambitious plans.

LOCKWOOD. What happened next?

CLEAVER. I started traveling.

LOCKWOOD. And you don't want to disclose where you went?

CLEAVER. Well, I feel that those whose business it really is, those who need to know in order to carry out some function of the struggle, they already have this information and they are acting on the basis of it. And those who are our friends and would like to know simply out of curiosity, well, they will have to wait. But those who want to know in order to carry out hostile acts on the basis of this information, they'll have to just seek a little harder in order to find that out. I'm not going to volunteer any information to J. Edgar Hoover. I know that he can get information very efficiently, but he will have to root for it. I am not going to help him at all.

LOCKWOOD. Last May, there was a report published in American newspapers that you had been living in Cuba for several months, surrounded by an "exile community of Black Panthers." After that, the U.S. Government declared that you were officially a resident of Cuba and that therefore none of the royalties from your books could any longer be paid to you, since Cuba falls under the "Trading with the Enemy" Act.

CLEAVER. I understand that the United States Government, on the basis of this Reuters report, has declared me to be a citizen of Cuba. I would assume from this that the United States Constitution is no longer available to me—if it ever was—so that I cannot invoke the Fifth Amendment. Therefore I will just say "no comment."

LOCKWOOD. Obviously you plan to stay outside the United States for an indefinite period of time. Do you have any specific plans as to where you will go?

CLEAVER. I assume you're speaking in terms of residence? There are many revolutionary countries around the world that would give sanctuary and security to a person in my position. I've been in several countries since leaving the United States, and I've talked to many people. I've done a lot of shopping around, and I'm not uptight about that at all. It's not a problem.

LOCKWOOD. Does being in exile make it difficult for you to maintain contact with your movement?

CLEAVER. Obviously, communications do become a little more difficult, a little more complex. There was a time when, for instance, I could pick up a telephone and talk to Bobby Seale. I could still do that right now, but for certain tactical reasons I don't. You might say that being in this position puts me out of some things and into some other things. There is still quite a bit that I am able to do that keeps me occupied. So I don't think that I will be in a position where I will atrophy and become nonfunctional. I think that I can continue to contribute to making the American revolution.

LOCKWOOD. As you know, a large number of Panthers have been arrested lately in various cities across the

United States. Many of them have been given inflated bail amounts. Do you see a pattern in these arrests?

CLEAVER. There is no question in my mind that there's a blueprint—a conspiratorial blueprint—that's being unfolded by the Nixon administration, spearheaded by the FBI. We can no longer talk of "inflated bail" being imposed on the people who are being arrested. We have to start talking about ransom, because when you start placing $100,000 bail or $200,000 bail, while the United States Constitution says that unreasonable bail shall not be imposed, what you're doing is just publicly throwing the Constitution into the wastebasket. Prohibitive bails have been placed against black people in the past, so this is really a quantitative change. But it's also a qualitative change. Two hundred thousand dollars bail for some poor cat out of the ghetto, unemployed—that's ransom. So there is no doubt that there is a conscious and well-planned attempt to destroy the Black Panther Party in progress right now.

It is only because it's just beginning to make headlines that more people are becoming aware of this. But we were aware of the desire of the power structure to eliminate the Black Panther Party as far back as 1966, when it first got started in Oakland, California. It was immediately met with unprecedented hostility from the power structure, particularly from the police departments. The first real overt action to destroy the Black Panther Party—a very serious act—was when they moved against Huey P. Newton. They tried to kill Huey. They did shoot him, and then they railroaded him through the courts. Now, the trial of Huey Newton was held in the full light of day. It's on record; you can read the transcripts, and a lot of people have written about it besides, so you can look into it and see that Huey was railroaded into prison. I don't want to rehash the entire situation. But we say that the persecution and overt repression of the Black Panther Party started when they moved against the leader of the Party. And it has not only continued, it has *escalated*. They seem to want to pick off the leadership of the Black Panther Party in hopes that the whole Party will just disintegrate.

As a matter of fact, it's been my experience that every time they have made a heavy move against the Party, it has grown. The first great leap in membership was in May 1967, when we visited the California State Legislature and twenty-four members were arrested because we went there with guns. When we got out of jail, the membership of the Party had increased dramatically. Then, in October 1967, following the incident in which Huey P. Newton was jailed, the Party moved from a local organization into a nationwide organization. And again, in April of last year, following the incident in which Bobby Hutton was killed and I was shot and then arrested, the Party experienced another leap in membership. It is clear from an analysis of how revolutionary movements develop that people who are standing around watching and sympathizing but who haven't made a decision as to whether they are going to be part of the problem or part of the solution are kind of pulled into the situation each time they see another flagrant example of the persecution against which we are struggling. So I feel that all of this blatant persecution, these open fascistic police tactics under the Nixon administration, will not only swell the membership of the Black Panther Party but will increase the ranks of all radical and revolutionary organizations in the United States, because people will recognize that if such things can be done in the black community, they can be done in the white community too.

LOCKWOOD. Recently, the McClellan Subcommittee of the Senate has been investigating the activities of the Black Panther Party in the United States. Have you heard about the young couple who identified themselves as Black Panthers and testified that they had been ordered to commit robberies for the Panthers?

CLEAVER. Yes, I've kept informed about what's going on.
Here we have Senator John McClellan, the head of the Committee, who, by the way, is from my home state of Arkansas, the state of Orville Faubus, you know, and this racist pig, who holds an illegal seat in the Senate by virtue of the disenfranchisement of black people in his state, a man who is a political criminal, is conducting these investigations. What they're doing is trying to buy time, because they see that the people are rising up against them, and they want to stage a circus, using their hired flunkies who infiltrated the Black Panther Party and then took this position in order to discredit and offer some justification for suppressing the Black Panther

Party. This is like everything else they do these days. It's like the war in Vietnam, you know. They conducted this war, and they came out and lied about it; they tried to justify it, but it continued to fall apart. They said they would never negotiate, they would never even recognize what they call the Viet Cong, but now they're sitting down in Paris and they're talking to them. Now, this investigation, to my mind, is the same thing, in that it is a form of recognition that they're giving to the Black Panther Party and to the other groups that they're investigating. Mao Tse-tung, in his little Red Book, says that sometimes it's good to be attacked by the enemy, because you create a clear line of demarcation between yourself and the enemy. So I think what they're doing will have the opposite effect to what they want to achieve, because when such odious characters say such bad things about an organization, there is an automatic process of reversing the symbolism, particularly on the part of an oppressed people. The oppressed people will know that the Black Panther Party must be doing something good, because the bad people are mad and are moving against the Party.

LOCKWOOD. The Black Panther Party seems to have a bad image in the American press as a whole. For example, the press gave a lot of coverage to that couple's story that fourteen-year-old girls were being ordered to submit sexually to Panther men, and that they themselves had even been locked up in a "Black Panther jail" in Oakland, California. One reads and hears many stories of this kind about the Panthers. Why do you think the Panthers have such a bad press?

CLEAVER. I think that when you talk about the image that is reflected in the "press," you have to realize that the press is controlled by the exploiters, by the ruling class. But if you look at the press of the people, which we refer to as the underground press, you will find just the reverse; you'll find that the Panthers have a very good image in the underground press and that these persecutors, these witch hunters, have a very bad image in the press of the people. In the press of the pigs, yes, we have a bad image; but if we had a good image, if they were to talk about us the way they talk about Roy Wilkins and the NAACP and all those bootlickers and Uncle Toms and black capitalists, then I would be gravely concerned.

I don't know those two individuals personally, because they were not there when I was there. They came along, as I understand it, just long enough to put on a black leather jacket and a black beret and a black shirt in order to show up in Washington in time to testify. But I know that the testimony that they gave is carefully calculated to undermine us.

For instance, they said that the Black Panther Party extorted from merchants in order to get the goods to provide breakfasts for children. Now, the Panthers have a breakfasts-for-children program, where, in fact, the Party is speaking to the real needs of the people. There were thousands of children in the ghetto who were not receiving breakfasts every morning. So the Black Panther Party established this program, and you can call it extortion if you want to, but the Party goes around to the merchants who exploit the black community and demands from these merchants that they contribute something to this program. They do this very vigorously, and the merchants, since they're greedy and they want to sell their products and make a profit, resent this and say that the Black Panthers are extorting them. But the Black Panthers are getting back from them something that they are stealing from the people.

But you see, they are making all these charges about young girls being sexually abused in order to cast discredit on the program. And this is just one example of how the testimony is carefully rigged. If you would take a look, if you would just go down into the black community, you would see a host of beautiful girls, and if you asked them what kind of boy friend they like, they would not tell you that they like a bootlicker or an Uncle Tom; they would say "Give me a Black Panther." So these are just ridiculous charges. The Black Panthers are not in a position where they have to get their kicks from fooling around with children.

LOCKWOOD. But is it a Panther policy to tell somebody to take a gun and go hold up a store?

CLEAVER. If you listen, you will not hear anyone saying that it is a Panther policy except those who are saying it at the behest of the pigs and to help the pigs. So just listen to what the Panthers are saying. The Panthers are saying that these are flunkies and tools of the power structure, and I think that's clear, because they are performing a service for the power structure, and they are not Panthers.

LOCKWOOD. How large is the Black Panther Party now?

CLEAVER. Nobody knows. I'm quite sure that there is nobody in the United States, from the FBI to Huey P. Newton, who could tell you precisely the number of members in the Black Panther Party.

LOCKWOOD. Well, approximately?

CLEAVER. I wouldn't even want to say approximately, because I've recently been reunited with my wife * and I was not in detailed contact with her for these months, so I was not really in a position to keep up on such things as statistics of growth in the Party. But from what she tells me, the Party is enjoying unprecedented support in the community; it is growing stronger and increasing in membership. I read in the papers now about new branches that didn't exist while I was in the United States. I remember one day I picked up a newspaper and I read about the office of the Black Panther Party in Des Moines, Iowa, being blown up by a bomb. And when I was there we didn't even have a branch in Des Moines, Iowa. So I am not in a position to say how many Panthers there are, but there are enough there to interest J. Edgar Hoover and Senator McClellan and Richard Milhous Nixon.

* Kathleen Cleaver, Eldridge's wife, is Communications Secretary of the Black Panther Party.

The only thing we can say is that, speaking historically, in October 1966 there were only two Panthers—Bobby Seale and Huey P. Newton, when they founded the organization. Since that time, I'm not sure if *they* have ever known what the precise number was. I know that the Black Panther Party is now a nationwide organization with chapters in every large city where there is a large number of black people. I know that we have chapters in the South. We even have a chapter in Halifax, Nova Scotia. I am very proud of that. If I knew exactly how many there were, I wouldn't have any tactical reason for not telling you. But all I can say is that we have a large national organization with thousands of members; I don't know if it's 100,000 members or 10,000 or 20,000 or 30,000. I know that there are thousands in the state of California and I believe that there are thousands in the state of New York, but I don't know exactly how many. I would like the Black Panther Party to include every black person in the United States.

LOCKWOOD. Then you want it to be a mass organization?

CLEAVER. I think there is a need for the masses to be organized. But this creates certain problems. From its inception, the Black Panther Party has been a vanguard organization. And a vanguard organization inevitably undergoes a change at the point where it achieves its purpose of organizing the people, or at least at the point where, by setting an example, it succeeds in getting the people to accept its political leadership. When that point is reached, the vanguard has a responsibility of creating machinery by which it can both function as a vanguard and include the masses in organizational structure. So that there are inevitable changes that have to be made. Actually, I feel that the Black Panther Party has already reached a point where such structural changes are indicated. There have been such a large number of people involved, while at the same time the repression of the power structure has become so great, that it will not be long before we will have to modify our approach to things in order to continue to be effective and to offset the escalation of the repression of the power structure.

The reason that the Party has developed and functioned in the manner that it has grows out of a decision made by Huey Newton. In one of his essays, entitled "The Correct Handling of the Revolution," Huey pointed out the necessity of the vanguard organization starting to function above ground. At the inception of the Party, he and Bobby Seale had a discussion with other individuals about whether you started underground or above ground, particularly since the Party related to using guns as the tool of liberation. These individuals wanted to start underground because they were afraid to confront the cops openly with guns. But Huey and Bobby felt that this was an erroneous tactic, that by starting underground you acknowledged a sort of defeat, you eschewed your legitimacy. In the first place, revolutionaries have nothing to hide; that which is hidden is done so only out of the tactical necessity of eluding the pigs. Huey felt that it was necessary to start above ground so that the people would know that the Party existed and so that they could educate the people. You could not organize a secret organization and then pass out leaflets at night telling the people that you existed and that they should do this and that, or that they should even listen to you at all. Huey felt that you had to be visible and let your actions speak for themselves, and that when the time came when you were driven underground, the people would know that you still existed and there would be a transference of the credibility that your organization gained above ground.

I feel that we have now reached the point where we have to develop the other aspect of a classic structure of a revolutionary movement: that is, the distinction between a political arm and a military arm that is necessary in order to develop a people's war. Because we are functioning in an urban situation, it is necessary for us to create this type of machinery at this point in our struggle.

LOCKWOOD. You mean a political leadership separate from the military leadership?

CLEAVER. Yes. Just *how* separate is nobody's business. But in terms of being able to confront the power structure, in terms of what they're able to blame on the aboveground aspect of the apparatus, I think it's necessary to make it very difficult for them to do that.

LOCKWOOD. Are you familiar with Regis Debray's book *Revolution in the Revolution?* Applying the example of the Cuban revolution, Debray rejects the separation of military and political functions in the revolutionary vanguard. He says they are one and the same, that the military leadership during the guerrilla phase of a revolution must become the political leadership when the revolution comes to power.

Do you think that the examples of other revolutions can be applied to the situation in the United States?

CLEAVER. The leaders of the Black Panther Party have paid very close attention to the experiences of other revolutionaries. We are aware of these theories, particularly the experience in Latin America, and we feel that our situation is unique, just as Regis Debray and Che Guevara and Fidel Castro were advancing theories that applied to a unique situation. We feel that it is necessary to take general classical revolutionary principles and apply them to our specific situation. And the specific situation that exists in the United States is not the same situation that has existed in other places. So we cannot follow the model of the Bolshevik Revolution, we cannot follow the model of the Chinese Revolution, we cannot follow the model of the Cuban Revolution, but we can gain from the experiences of all of these.

I am saying that we have to elaborate a theory that will cope with the highly urbanized, highly mechanized, industrialized society that we live in. There has never been a revolution made in the type of society that I speak of. And I don't think that the *foco* theory as elaborated by Debray, principally by Debray but as taken from Guevara and Fidel, specifically applies to the situation in the United States. I do think that the essential dynamics of the *foco* theory apply anywhere where there is vanguard activity of the type spoken of in Debray's works. This is something that has happened in terms of what the Black Panther Party has been doing—but they have not been doing it in the mountains.

I am very critical of what I call "revolutionary romanticism." I'm talking about people in the United States who have been relating to all of those wall posters and paintings of the guerrillas from the mountains and then find themselves walking around the cities in combat boots and fatigue jackets. I understand what they are doing. They're trying to identify with proven revolutionaries. But, unfortunately, this is not functional in an urban situation.

I say that it would be more functional for revolutionaries in the urban situation to study the model of the Mafia to see how they move in the cities, because they function in terms of arms in an organized fashion. How can you swim like a fish through the water, as Mao said you should move through the masses—how can you move through the masses in combat boots? Instead, you should think about how the criminal element functions in Babylon. When a guy goes out to rob a bank, he doesn't go out dressed like Robin Hood or a Mexican bandit. He would probably go dressed like a businessman, because he wants to blend with his surroundings. So those who function in urban guerrilla warfare have a responsibility to take a look at the terrain. We need to develop a concept of urban geography, because the only models of revolutionary behavior that we have are those taken from rural geography and rural terrain. We could really make terrible mistakes and lose a lot of lives unnecessarily by adopting coldbloodedly the theories of revolutionary struggle that has been waged under different circumstances and conditions, mainly in rural areas of underdeveloped countries with a different type of military establishment.

For instance, I found in Babylon that one of the most serious things that we have to deal with is the communications and mobility of the police departments. You have to deal with that anywhere where you engage in struggle. But in the urban situation this becomes key. Communications, mobility and electricity—lights. We have to think in terms of what we're confronted with and then we know what counter strategy we have to devise.

LOCKWOOD. Why do you say "Babylon"?

CLEAVER. Because of all the symbols that I've ever run across to indicate a decadent society, I find the term Babylon, which I take from Revelations in the Bible, to be the most touching. That's how they describe Babylon —as a decadent society. *Fuck* the Bible. I don't want to peddle the Bible. But it comes out of the Bible anyway, out of Revelations.

LOCKWOOD. It's an analogue?

CLEAVER. It's an analogue. The United States of America is described in Revelations. I'm not being a prophet. I'm just saying that I dig that.

LOCKWOOD. When Martin Luther King died, you wrote that this is the end of nonviolence and the bloody struggle starts now; there is going to be a bloodbath and a guerrilla war. And one would gather from what you have been saying here that the Black Panthers are laying plans for guerrilla warfare in the United States. Why do you think that a guerrilla war is absolutely necessary at this time?

CLEAVER. Well, I don't like the way you ask that question, you see. Because you ask me, is the Black Panther Party laying plans for that? I just want to say that this is my belief, and this is what is going on in my mind, and this is what I feel is necessary, and this is what I am dedicated to, and this is what I know a lot of other people are dedicated to, and this is what I feel that all revolutionaries in the United States should be dedicated to—to recognize that we have to fight a revolutionary struggle for the violent overthrow of the United States government and the total destruction of the racist, capitalist, imperialist, neo-colonialist power structure. This is what I'll be working on henceforth: to establish the North American Liberation Front, which will include the revolutionary forces in every community. It will not be an all-black organization; it will be a machinery that will include the revolutionaries in the white community, of the Mexican-American community, the Chinese community, the Puerto Rican community and the black community. The experience we have gained in the Black Panther Party, particularly in developing our coalition for working with revolutionaries in other communities, must now be transferred over, not into the political arena, but strictly into the military arena where politics have been transformed into warfare. And this is what I see the whole situation moving into, and this is what I'm pushing for, and this is what I have been working on ever since I have left Babylon.

LOCKWOOD. Late last year, in an interview just before you disappeared, you said: "It may still be possible, barely possible, to revolutionize this society to get fundamental structural changes without resorting to civil war, but only if we get enough power before it's too late." Have you changed your mind since then—do you now think it is too late for peaceful changes?

CLEAVER. I don't think there is any contradiction or change in my position, because I've always moved from an analysis of the American system. What I said in that interview, and what I'm saying now, is that if the United States government would change the structure of the country so that people would no longer be oppressed, so that people would no longer be subjected to all the grievances about which we complain, then obviously the fuel for the fire would not be there. But obviously, the way that the situation has developed, there has been more fuel added to the fire. What I'm saying now is that things have gone so far that there is a conflagration indicated. As far as I'm concerned there can be nothing *but* the conflagration. The very nature of the capitalistic system is such—I've always felt this, you see—that I have never had any hope that the United States of America could make peaceful modifications or that it could be perpetuated in the future in its present condition.

I'm saying to you that I feel that the United States as it exists today has to be totally obliterated and has to be rebuilt and restructured, and the wealth, the means of production, the entire system, has to be rearranged. And it won't be rearranged peacefully, because it's clear that those who control the United States have no intention whatsoever of modifying what's going on there, that in fact what they are doing is escalating the repression against the forces that are moving for change. The only fitting response to this repression can be implacable resistance, and the only implacable resistance that can possibly be manifested in this situation is open warfare against the system.

LOCKWOOD. Nevertheless, you did say in that interview that there might still be time for peaceful changes to occur in American society to avoid the "conflagration" you are talking about, whereas now you are saying that the conflagration is "inevitable." Is it possible that your thinking has become more radical since you left the United States?

CLEAVER. Well, there are a lot of relationships that I had a year ago which I no longer have. For instance, the relationship between myself and the power structure of the United States of America has been made crystal-clear. As far as they are concerned, I am a fugitive from justice. As far as *I* am concerned, *they* are fugitives from the justice of the people. So it is only a question of what forces can be mobilized to see who is the fugitive in the end. I intend to do everything I can to see to it that what I represent and what I advocate prevails. That may be speaking from a position of weakness in some people's eyes, but I feel that I am speaking from a position of strength. I don't believe that the revolutionary forces in the United States of America are faced with a crisis; I think that the United States itself, the structure and the system of the United States, is the entity that is faced with a crisis, and that I represent part of that crisis, and I intend to do everything I can to aggravate that crisis. I have broken off relationships with them; I don't belong to them; I am not their property. They can call me their fugitive; I call them my fugitives. They want to arrest me; I want to arrest them. They want to execute me; I want to execute them. So it's only a question of who will be executed and who will be captured, you see. And I have not been captured yet, and I have not been executed yet; I have not captured them yet and I have not executed them yet; but they are still trying and I am still trying, and I don't know how the shit is going to end, and I don't give a fuck, but I am going to be trying.

LOCKWOOD. But you are outside the country. Don't you find it a little hard to conduct this struggle, being so far away?

CLEAVER. No, no, no! Our struggle in the United States is not an isolated struggle. I have always been an internationalist. I think that any true revolutionary has to be an internationalist, because our oppressor has an international system. Racism, imperialism, capitalism, colonialism and neo-colonialism are international. All these oppressors are united on the international level in every organization from the United States to NATO, you see. And they function hand in hand. The racists who oppress black people in the United States work hand in hand with the racists in Portugal and in South Africa and in every backward, decadent system in the world. So that one can fight no matter where one is in the world. But I'm saying this: while I have full sympathy with those who struggle in every nook and cranny of the world, I consider that my battlefront, the battlefront where I can make the best contribution because of my familiarity with it, is in Babylon. This is where I want to fight. This is where I want to die.

LOCKWOOD. That means that you will go back to the United States?

CLEAVER. That means I'm going back. That means that I have every intention of going back to the United States of America. I think that I will be able to do that. The pigs of the power structure, even though they tried their best, were not able to keep me from leaving, and they will not be able to keep me from re-entering. I will re-enter, and I plan to shed my blood and to put my life on the line and to seek to take the lives of the pigs of the power structure in Babylon. This is where I want to do my thing.

LOCKWOOD. When?

CLEAVER. Well, that's none of your business. I cannot say that to you, you know.

LOCKWOOD. Do you yourself know when it will be?

CLEAVER. Well, I have a timetable. But obviously this is not something that we talk about in an interview.

LOCKWOOD. In your book *Soul on Ice,* you wrote: "From my prison cell I had watched America slowly coming awake. It is not fully awake yet but there is soul in the air and everywhere I see beauty." And in many other instances you have spoken about the United States in a way that indicates that you take a certain pride in being an American. Even though you've been informed that you are no longer a United States citizen, do you still *feel* that you are an American?

CLEAVER. Well, I would not like this to be like my definitive statement on that subject, because that obviously requires a lot of thought. But just off the top of my head: yes, I would like to say that I am an American. I'm an Afro-American, but I know that I share the experiences and the history of the American people. I feel patriotic. I feel that I am a super-patriot, but not to the America I left.

You see, I believe that there are two Americas. There is the America of the American dream, and there is the America of the American nightmare. I feel that I am a citizen of the American dream, and that the revolutionary struggle of which I am a part is a struggle against the American nightmare, which is the present reality. It is the struggle to do away with this nightmare and to replace it with the American dream which should be the reality. I have always said that the basic problem in America is confusion. I know I am an American; I am an Afro-

American, which means that I'm Afro and I'm also American. I know the American people, and I know the ideals that are instilled in one. I know how they are imbedded in the heart, you see. You have to look at the process of the formation of the American character structure, look at the children in American grammar schools and high schools and look at the ideals that are implanted in them there.

The children of America are the ones I consider to be the citizens of the American dream. First this foundation, all these ideals—the Bill of Rights, the Constitution and the Rights of Man, the Lord's Prayer, all of these things that no one can really attack, these things that have inspired people everywhere—are implanted in the hearts and the minds of the children of America. This is the foundation of the American character. But here is when the trick comes in. Later on, these ideals are twisted to function in behalf of a vicious power structure and a vicious economic and political and social system. My quarrel is against what is done with this foundation that has been instilled in people, and this is a very important distinction to make. Because what happens to people in the United States is that they are given these dreams and then they are put through a very subtle process of twisting and deformation and brainwashing, and they really have no defenses against this process because it's done by a very elaborate structure. And the dream is very subtly transformed into a nightmare.

LOCKWOOD. What exactly is the American dream you believe in? How would you define it?

CLEAVER. I believe that the American dream is that just as it says, "that all men are created equal, and that they are endowed by their creator"—I mean, I don't believe in God, you know, but I understand what the thought is—"that they are endowed by their Creator with certain inalienable rights, and that among these are the rights of life, liberty and the pursuit of happiness." And not the pursuit of property, which was struck from that.

It's very significant that Huey P. Newton made as an appendage to the Ten Point Program and Platform of the Black Panther Party a section from the Declaration of Independence of the United States that talks about all of this. He appended that because he understood, as every revolutionary in the United States has always understood, that he was struggling and fighting to implement that dream. It's possible to be confused on this issue. But it's very important not to be confused and to understand that.

For instance, take the Pledge of Allegiance to the flag. I remember as a child how I used to choke up every morning—we used to have to line up and pledge allegiance to the flag, you know. And we'd say things like "I pledge allegiance to the flag of the United States of America, and to the Republic for which it stands, one nation indivisible, with liberty and justice for all." Now it didn't say "I pledge allegiance to racism, to capitalism, and to the war in Vietnam, and to imperialism and neo-colonialism, and J. Edgar Hoover, and Richard Nixon, and Ronald Reagan, and Mayor Alioto, and the Tactical Squad, and Mace, and billy clubs, and dead niggers on the street shot by pigs." I mean it didn't say that shit, you see. So what I'm saying is that people have these ideals instilled in their hearts and it becomes part of their character structure. And then later on, the educational system, newspapers, magazines, radio, television, *Newsweek, Time* magazine, *Life* magazine, they tell you that "I pledge allegiance to all these things." And pretty soon, like you hate the man sitting next to you, you know, and you feel that you have to go and kill this person, that it's your patriotic duty, because somehow the profits of General Motors are tied up with the Bill of Rights. And the shit gets all fucked up and twisted up and you end up in the John Birch Society. But that's not what that's all about, that's not what the child is taught, you see. That's not what is instilled in the heart. I'm saying that our struggle is to make a demarcation between the dream and the nightmare. And that's all I'm saying, and that's all I ever want to say, because that's all that is important, you see. And okay, I'm not a citizen of the United States of America according to those who are citizens of the nightmare, but according to those who are citizens of the dream I'm a citizen in good standing, and I don't give a fuck what J. Edgar Hoover or Richard Nixon says.

LOCKWOOD. Assuming that the coalition of revolutionary forces you mentioned can actually take power, what are the structural means by which the nightmare that you speak of could be transformed into the dream that you wish for?

CLEAVER. What we seek, and what the world seeks, and what has been the dream of mankind, is utopia. Now, utopia has been turned into a dirty word. Like, when you stigmatize something, you call it "utopia." But is there really anything wrong with utopia? You know, utopia is a beautiful term.

LOCKWOOD. That's like asking is there anything wrong with heaven.

CLEAVER. Right, that's what that says. And what we want to do is to bring heaven down to earth, you see. That is, to create the best possible living conditions and standards of living that human knowledge and technology are capable of providing. That's the aspiration of the revolutionary, and that's the dream. So I'm saying that ideologically our hope indicates a socialist America, a communist America. Now you can get involved and quibble over terms. I'm not saying a Russian America; I'm not saying a Chinese America; I'm not saying a Cuban America; I'm saying an American application of the principles of socialism that hopes to move to the class-less society.

I'm saying that we have to make a specific application of the general principles of socialism to the American situation and come up with a Yankee-Doodle-Dandy version of socialism, one that will fit our particular situation. I'm saying that we have to do away with the institution of private property. I'm saying that justice requires and demands, the situation requires and demands, that we have an equal distribution of the products of our industry and our technology. I'm saying that the problems that exist in the United States today are not economic problems.

We have no economic problems in the United States—we have political problems. I'm saying that what we need to do is to rearrange the system. And a rearrangement of the system in the United States would do away with the grievances, because we have productivity up the ass. I mean we have abundance up the ass. There is no need for anyone to be talking about a war on poverty, for instance, in the United States of America. What we need in the United States is a war on the rich. We need a war on the system of the rich. We need a war on the system that allows poverty to exist in the midst of all those riches. So what I'm saying is that since the earth is given, and since Rockefeller didn't slide from his mother's womb with any blue-chip stocks, since everyone comes here in the same manner, since everyone has life and in store for everyone is death——and I don't believe that there is any heaven involved, that if there is going to be any heaven it's going to have to be right here on earth——I'm saying that we all deserve to have the benefit of all of human history, the cumulative benefit of the development of technology and human wisdom. And the only way that I can understand that this could really be done is through a system that says that Rockefeller doesn't own all the oil in the world and that General Motors doesn't own an exclusive patent on the rights to transportation. I'm saying that everyone has a right to these things and that we need a system that guarantees to everybody the right to access on an equal basis to all that it takes to make up the good life, and that this has to be socialism. Where the means of production belong to everybody. Where no one is in a position to exclude any-one else from the good life. Where no one is able to say, well you can't have this because I own it. Where no one can say that this mountain of iron belongs to me because my father was a robber baron and he bequeathed it to me. I'm saying that all that shit is a part of the past. I'm saying that we need to close the book on the America of the nightmare. This is what I refer to as the history "of the pigs, for the pigs, and by the pigs." I'm saying that, so you inherited this from your father or your grand-father who stole it from the Indians, so you have this shit written on paper—I'm saying that that paper can be burnt. I'm saying that we need to have if necessary another constitutional convention, where another under-standing can be made, because there is great disagree-ment in the land. And what I advocate is the total, un-equivocal destruction of capitalism and in its place a socialist system that would be compatible with the spirit of the American people. That would be calculated to apply specifically to conditions that exist in the United States of America. That will not turn the United States of America into a satellite of the Soviet Union, that will not turn the American people into Chinese people or into Cuban people, but that will put the American people on a basis where they can be friends with the peo-ple in the Soviet Union, with the people in China, with the people in Cuba, in fact with the people of the whole world.

I think that this can be done by rearranging the system to eliminate the antagonisms between the people in the

United States and the people in these other areas. For instance, who has an interest in having an antagonistic relationship to the people in Vietnam? I don't. The average man in the United States doesn't. I mean, how do you get from the Pledge of Allegiance to the battlefield of Vietnam? That's a very complicated process, and I'm saying that you have to go throughout the economic system and the political system and the social system and all the lies before you can remove yourself from a position with your hand over your heart pledging allegiance to the flag, talking about liberty and justice for all, and then finding yourself over in Vietnam shooting people. I mean, there is a lot of shit that you have to go through before you move from one point to the other. And I'm saying that this shit that you have to move through is capitalism and racism and exploitation and all of this. And I'm saying that we can remove this by eliminating the present system in the United States and by recognizing that by removing this system, life does not end, that we do not lose face by doing this. This is progress, this is good, because we go from something that we have now, something that we have had, to something that is better. It's like going from slavery to segregation. I think that any slave would say that, like slavery was a bad scene, but segregation was better. And segregation is a bad scene, but integration is better. I am saying that integration is a bad scene and that freedom and liberty is better, you see. I'm saying that slavery on the economic level is a bad scene, that capitalism is a bad scene, and that socialism is better.

LOCKWOOD. Well, assuming that this dream is realizable, what you haven't done is proposed a model or a system by which it could be realized. You've spoken in general terms, and it may be that you can't yet speak of specific things—

CLEAVER. What are you talking about that I can't speak in specifics? I'm saying that we overthrow the government and then we nationalize Standard Oil, you see?

LOCKWOOD. Well what I'm getting at—I have a question that's behind what I started to say.

CLEAVER. What is the question, you know?

LOCKWOOD. You mentioned the Soviet Union, China and Cuba, three countries which have had socialist revolutions at different times: one fifty years ago, one twenty years ago, one ten years ago. In each of these countries, the economic resources have been nationalized, capitalism has been largely or totally done away with, and there has been a redistribution of wealth, a leveling of privilege and a restructuring of the society more or less along the lines you're discussing. Now, in terms of the kind of socialist society that you hope to see in the United States, do you feel satisfied about the results in any one of the three countries that you mentioned?

CLEAVER. No. On certain levels, yes. There are good things that have happened in all of those countries. But I believe that consciousness is very important at this point. And I believe that consciousness has been expanded in the United States of America beyond the consciousness possessed by any other people on the face of the planet Earth. Now, I don't know what kind of trouble I might get myself into for saying that, but this is what I believe.

LOCKWOOD. I don't understand. Are you saying that consciousness has expanded among all the people of the United States?

CLEAVER. No, no, I mean we have idiots, we have idiots like Richard Nixon in the United States, all right? I say that Richard Nixon is an underdeveloped cretin—a political and a moral cretin—so that his consciousness is pinched and not expanded. I don't know where we went to, but we got away from your original question.

LOCKWOOD. The question is: Are you satisfied with any of the three models that you alluded to?

CLEAVER. Not *in toto*. But I think that every country has to do its own thing, you know? I don't think that you can just blindly follow the model.

I'm not satisfied with anything that exists on the face of the planet Earth today. I think that in some respects the Cuban experience is the most relevant to our experience in the United States, because in the United States and in Cuba you have a certain thing that's very essential; that is, you have black people and you have white people. And how Cuba has moved to solve this problem is very important. This is a subject that I've paid close attention to for many years, and it seems to me that of all the white people that exist on the face of the planet Earth, the white people of Cuba were making the greatest effort to do something positive about this. It was for that reason that for me and for many black people the Cuban revolution was of paramount importance. It was of paramount importance even to Malcolm X. When Fidel Castro came to the United Nations, Malcolm X—who was then still a follower of Elijah Muhammad—was very happy to meet with Fidel when Fidel went to the Hotel Theresa in Harlem after being persecuted from a hotel downtown by the white folks. Malcolm X at that time was willing to go down and shake hands with Fidel and embrace him and have his picture taken smiling with him. For both black people and white people in the United States, the Cuban revolution has been very important. Not because of the economic reforms of the revolution—I think that's a secondary consideration for North Americans—but because of what is being done in terms of dealing with the racial problem. That's what's important, because that's what *we* have to deal with. Because in the United States of America we don't have just an economic problem, it's not just a question of the antagonism between the bourgeoisie and the proletariat; we also have antagonism between ethnic groups. That is very important.

LOCKWOOD. In your book *Soul on Ice* there is an essay called "Domestic Law and International Order," in which you criticize governmental power structures in general, both capitalist and communist. You say: "Which laws get enforced depends on who is in power. If the capitalists are in power, they enforce laws designed to protect their system, their way of life. They have a particular abhorrence for crimes against property, but are prepared to be liberal and show a modicum of compassion for crimes against the person, etc." Then you criticize the communist system. You say: "If Communists are in power, they enforce laws designed to protect their system, their way of life. To them, the horror of horrors is the speculator, that man of magic who has mastered the art of getting something with nothing and who in America would be a member in good standing of his local Chamber of Commerce." And you go on in the next paragraph: " 'The people,' however, are nowhere consulted, although everywhere everything is done always in their name and ostensibly for their betterment, while their real-life problems go unsolved. 'The people' are a rubber stamp for the crafty and sly."

When you wrote those words some three years ago, you seemed to have equally harsh criticisms of both capitalism and communism. Should one conclude that you feel differently about communism now?

CLEAVER. No. I have more information on the subject now, but I still have my criticisms as to how communism is being organized in various places. I don't think this is anything surprising, because people within communist countries also have criticisms about the way they've been organized. The point is that under capitalism, as far as I'm concerned, the people are unrepresented. In the United States we have what you call representative democracy, but it's pretty clear that the system is a rigged system. Even though it is called a "government of the people and by the people," the people are not really in a position to determine what is going to happen. They do not control the decision-making process.

I don't think that a perfect machinery has been worked out anywhere in the world under which the people are able to participate smoothly and *in toto* in the decision-making process. I think that no system will be perfect. I would not certify any system as being finalized or ideal until it discovers a way that every man can have his opinions taken into consideration when decisions are being arrived at. This is a very important point, and we must not become complacent and accept anything less than that.

At the time that I wrote that chapter of my book, my preference for communism as opposed to capitalism was very clear in my mind. But I don't want to be in the position of saying that after the capitalist state is done away with and the communists are in power, all problems cease to exist. I don't think there are any communists in the world who will claim that. But I would not condemn communism with the same emphasis that I would condemn capitalism, because I prefer communism to capitalism. What I do condemn very strongly is all structural imperfections. What we are trying to do is to improve the condition of humanity and to do away with all the structural entities that keep people uptight. As long as there is a single man in the Soviet Union or China or Cuba whose position in the political structure is such that his will is not taken into the balance along with everyone else's will, as long as that situation exists in one iota, one degree, there's work to be done and I condemn that one degree vigorously.

You must understand that Marxism has never really been given a chance in this world. Every country that has tried to establish a socialist system has been a country under siege. When the Soviet Union was transformed into a socialist country after the revolution, it was subjected to a blockade and an invasion by foreign troops sent by capitalism and imperialism. In every country which has tried it, the whole process of developing a socialist system has been distorted by security considerations, because each one has had to divert a large portion of its resources into armaments in order to defend itself against the aggressions of capitalism. They have had to maintain very tight systems of security because of the unceasing efforts of the capitalists to overthrow their governments. All of these considerations serve to distort the true nature of socialism. Socialism seeks to implement an ideal. It needs an environment where it is not under a state of siege in order to develop all of its contours and to really have a chance to see whether it can work for the people.

So I'm saying that the key revolution that the world is waiting for is the American revolution, because America is the bastion of imperialism; it is the hub of all of the oppressive forces in the world. If we can achieve a revolution in the United States and disrupt and destroy all of the awesome structures that seek to interfere with people in their attempt to develop their social and poli-

tical and economic systems, then I think that the resources which will be released from all of these military
and security considerations will go a long way toward
establishing the kind of system that everyone can respect.

LOCKWOOD. Based on your studies of societies which
have already undergone socialist revolutions, how do you
think it will be possible to construct a socialist system in
the United States in which an elite power structure will
not be evolved which will manipulate the people? What
are the lessons that can be learned from the evolution of
communist societies so far in contemporary history, and
how do you think they can be applied to the situation in
the United States?

CLEAVER. I was trying to get into this earlier when I was
talking about the consciousness of the American people.
There's something very important about the history of
revolution in the world, and that is that the United States
of America was the first country that liberated itself from
colonialism in this epoch that we live in. So that the
American people have been imbued with a spirit of
liberty. They have a very deep respect for the individual
and for the rights of the individual. A lot of other countries, particularly those that have become communist,
have not had a history of democracy as we have known
it in the United States. The Soviet Union, for instance,
was under a Czarist dictatorship, and China was under
the dynasties of emperors for thousands of years, and
you have Cuba—these are not the only socialist countries,
but they are the ones whose revolutions were relatively

independent, so that we can talk about them as offering some very distinct patterns. In Cuba, where there was a tradition of dictatorships with very little respect for the rights of the individual, the people have not possessed individual liberty to the extent that they really felt it was theirs, so that it is possible for a system to be imposed upon them under which they will not fight hard for that respect for the individual which we in the United States feel is so dear. I believe that with a socialist system in the United States we will create another synthesis of this experience. And I think that it will not be possible for a system to be imposed upon the American people that will completely deny all rights to the individual, because the American people are such that they will not go for this. They will not go for this.

LOCKWOOD. Do you really believe that there has been a history of democracy in the United States?

CLEAVER. There have been periods of stability.

Now, when you start talking about what's wrong with the United States, you also have to take into consideration the fact that everything that happens in the United States happens on a level far beyond what's happening in the rest of the world. Take poverty, for instance. Poverty in the United States cannot be talked about in the same sense that poverty can be talked about in India. I mean, you don't have people in the United States literally, and by the thousands, just starving to death. You have other forms of the dehumanization of the individual. You have other forms of the poverty of individuals. . . .

LOCKWOOD. Well, we also have Appalachia.

CLEAVER. Yes, but you don't have people in Appalachia like you have people in New Delhi. There's no place in Babylon that can be equated with the poverty in the rest of the world. I mean, everything in Babylon is a different experience. For example, historically, there has been so much subtlety to oppression in the United States, whereas in the other parts of the world oppression is overt. I'm not just talking about black people. For black people the oppression has been more overt and more blatant. But you will even find a lot of black people in the United States who think that they are free. And this is because of the subtlety of the situation.

LOCKWOOD. Is there any one country which has had a revolution to which you feel particularly sympathetic in terms of the revolution that you hope to see in the United States?

CLEAVER. No. I don't feel more sympathetic to any one or the other. As I said earlier, I think that the Cuban revolution is very important to us in the United States because of the ethnic composition of Cuba. But in terms of the structure of the country itself, I would have to make a much more detailed study of all these countries before I could speak about that. What I'm making my study and my practice is how we can apply the principles of socialism to the United States of America. This cannot be done by importing the experiences of other countries without taking into consideration what's going on in the

United States. The Soviet Union, the People's Republic of China, and Cuba—in each of these countries they had to face problems when their revolutions came to power that the United States doesn't have: the problem of developing the economy, the problem of the scarcity of material goods which was so important to all three of these countries at the time of their revolutions. These are not problems in the United States—you see? So that I'm sure that the revolution in the United States will take a much different form than the revolutions in all those other countries.

LOCKWOOD. Do you conceive of a socialist system being instituted in the United States according to the democratic traditions of the Bill of Rights, the Constitution and—

CLEAVER. No, I think that we would need to revamp all of those. I think that the ideals contained in these documents are eternal. But obviously there's something wrong with the Constitution if it can say that people are entitled to all these rights and this is the document that's supposed to secure them these rights, and yet under this document these rights have not been secured. I'm saying that something else has to be done to secure these rights. The Constitution of the United States authorized a particular form of government that is related to a particular economic system. The Constitution doesn't authorize capitalism. It is the interpretation that the judges of the United States Supreme Court, for instance, have put on the Fourteenth Amendment that allows people to be secure in their property rights. It is things of this sort which have allowed the flexibility of the Constitution and the concept of the balance between the Supreme Court, the Congress and the Executive Branch of the government, etc.

The basic problem is the institution of private property. We have to deal with the economic system. If we did not have capitalism in the United States, the Supreme Court would have to render different types of decisions. So that we have to evolve institutions based on our historic experience that will represent a continuity of that experience but at the same time a qualitative change in the way that it is implemented.

II

LOCKWOOD. Eldridge, I'd like to ask you some questions about your own ideological development. Could you describe the various transformations that you've gone through in your thinking, starting as far back as you remember that you had political ideas?

CLEAVER. Well, I became something of a rebel before I became political, I think that's very clear. My early years were outlaw years, full of vandalism and petty crimes and so forth, so that before beginning to view things in any political perspective I was very hostile to the situation that I found myself in. That included the political system, except that I didn't relate to it in any political sense. I was just hostile; I guess you might say that I didn't relate to any kind of authority.

LOCKWOOD. How old were you at the time you are talking about?

CLEAVER. I guess it goes back to the time I was twelve years old. I started getting into trouble with authorities, juvenile problems, during my early years. So I developed a very hostile attitude, a rebellious attitude you might say, that ran pretty deep. But it was not until I went to prison that I really began to expand my perspective. This came from reading and talking to other convicts. In that situation you have a lot of time on your hands. You have the time to watch the news, you know, you look at television and read newspapers and magazines. Watching the things that go on outside of the prison becomes sort of a pastime of convicts. When I first went to prison in 1954, the civil rights struggle was very much in the news every day, and it was kind of natural for black inmates to relate to this news and to follow the struggle. It was like watching some panoramic scene unfolding, one that you are not really directly involved in, and yet you identify totally with the people because they are black people.

I can actually remember a time in those days when I thought that the NAACP was the greatest thing that had ever existed. I had read the life of DuBois and studied about Booker T. Washington and Walter White. I used to read all about these individuals who were involved in the struggle, and it seemed to me that they were great crusaders involved in a great undertaking. So that I began to follow the development of events, and I began to consider the political and social situation and to try to understand how that all related to me.

Of course, in prison you encounter individuals who have been at it much longer than you have, so that they understand much more than you do and they act as sort of *gurus* for convicts. When I went to prison the first time in 1954 I met a fellow who was really the one who started me to reading. His name was Pontifelt. I had several friends who had preceded me to prison, and when I got there they were sort of disciples of his. He had been in jail for twelve years. He had everybody hung up on the dialogues of Plato. His approach to this was very mystical, and he was very out of his mind in a certain sense. We used to go down to the library on Saturday and sit around and listen to him talk. He was very knowledgeable about the philosophers, and he would talk about them and tell us how we were very stupid and didn't know what was going on in the world, and that the only way that we could save ourselves was to read these books and to gain this knowledge. There was this whole mystical thing about him.

LOCKWOOD. How much formal education did you have before you went to prison?

CLEAVER. Very little. You have to realize that I went to prison twice. I went first for a short stay, and I think that at that time I had about a tenth-grade education. When I got out I didn't go back to high school. I didn't get my high school diploma until I returned to prison, you see. I got it in San Quentin.

Anyhow, at this particular time Pontifelt was interesting people in reading and we used to sit around the library. I remember now that he was a Rosicrucian. He used to subscribe to their magazine, and he would pass it around and we would try to understand this secret wisdom. So it was very exciting. We were eighteen years old and all of that, you know. We would try to understand it, and it wasn't satisfying to us, but it was enough to keep us hung up and to keep us reading and I remember him getting us to read the essays of Ralph Waldo Emerson. Like the one on self-reliance—he said that we had to get this.

LOCKWOOD. Emerson was very much influenced by Oriental philosophers.

CLEAVER. That was his bag, you see: Rosicrucianism, Pyramids and secret wisdom. But anyway, this had a great influence on me. While I was there and considering what I was going to do with myself—I remember once I was sent to solitary confinement for twenty-nine days. In solitary confinement they only give you the Bible to read, and at that particular time I didn't like to read the Bible, so I was put into a position where I had to do a little thinking, lying up there in the cell by myself. I made a little decision for myself that when I got out of solitary confinement I would quit wasting my time and become a little more serious, and I would read more and study more and try to get some fat on my head, that's how we used to say that.

So when I got out of solitary, I became a little more serious about reading, and I began to develop a political perspective. I started reading a lot of radical materials that were available in the prison library—the Communist Manifesto, I struggled with *Das Kapital,* there were a lot of books there that one could read. But all this just gave me encouragement in the attitude that I already had towards the system. I didn't really assimilate this material. A few years later, I went back and reread those things because I had become serious about them. But it was really when I returned to prison the next time that I became serious about the political system and how that related all the way down to the individual. That was in 1957.

LOCKWOOD. How old were you then?

CLEAVER. Twenty-two years old, I'll never forget that. Twenty-two years old. But it didn't happen the first year. I went through many changes, through the Black Muslim Movement, etc. They had people in San Quentin who had organized a branch of the Communist Party, you know. And we really did some absurd things, but we were trying to relate to what we considered to be the best way of doing things with the knowledge that we had.

LOCKWOOD. Did you join the Communist Party?

CLEAVER. Well I never did really join it, because I had disagreements with the cat who was proselytizing around there. He seemed like a madman in many ways. I guess in many ways we were all madmen. But there was something very nice about it. I related to it, and we had some good conversations. I learned a lot from all of that.

LOCKWOOD. How did you become a convert to Islam?

CLEAVER. There was a time when I looked askance at it and I didn't see where it had any positive contribution to make to black people in that situation. But when I was in prison the first time there was a friend of mine who was a boxer by the name of Butterfly, we used to call him. He was a little boxer, a lightweight or something, and he was a very hostile individual. He didn't relate to any kind of organized structures. But when I returned to prison I found him there, and now he was the Minister of the Muslim Mosque in San Quentin. In trying to understand what had happened to him, I became interested in what Islam was all about.

At that time it was very difficult for the Muslims to get their literature into the prison. Elijah Muhammad used to publish a weekly column in the Los Angeles *Herald Dispatch,* and one or two copies of the paper would manage to get inside the prison. I had a typewriter and a job that provided me with the opportunity and the time to do a little typing. So what the Muslims would do was to bring a copy of it to me and I would put it on a stencil, and then they would have it run off on a mimeograph machine either in the Protestant Chapel or they would sneak into the Captain's office or the hospital. So I used to type these articles, and while typing them I used to read them. I remember that at first I used to read them and laugh. But finally, I started reading them and digging them, you know—typing and digging what the man was saying.

Then I became very dissatisfied with the way I was functioning in prison. By this time I was a trusty. I was living in an honor wing—they call it the "West Block" in San Quentin. I had been there two or three years and I had a good clean record, so that I had a job where I would go and open all the doors for the other convicts. I was trusted with a key—not the key to the front gate, but the keys to those cells. It was kind of meaningless, except that they called it a trusty thing. But I became dissatisfied with that, and talking to the Muslims and considering the situation, reading and studying and thinking about the world and what was going on in the United States, I developed a great deal of respect for the courage that the Muslims displayed in prison. Because they were really heavily persecuted. They were being locked up in solitary confinement, and they were the only blacks in prison who stuck together. Other blacks would stand around and criticize them, and yet they were doing nothing, while these blacks were confronting the authorities there and standing up for their rights. This exercised an attraction for me. I felt that I wasn't doing my part, that I owed something to that effort, because I was there and other blacks were there, and the Muslims were complaining about specific grievances within the prison system itself, you see. I felt that everyone had a duty to participate in that because it was here and now. So I got involved in it, and pretty soon all the hangups that I had about relating to the Muslims evaporated, because what was the most important thing was the struggle, and this was a way of relating to it.

LOCKWOOD. Did you believe in the religious content of the Muslim ideology?

CLEAVER. At first I had great difficulty with it. For years I had thought of myself as an atheist and argued with myself as to whether I should call myself an atheist or an agnostic. I had gone through all those changes, you see.

So that when I encountered Allah and the teachings of the Honorable Elijah Muhammad, this presented certain problems and contradictions for me. But after making a study of what Mr. Muhammad was teaching, I related to it as a language and a system of symbols that allowed one to communicate certain things. To me, it was like learning a new language and how to talk these symbols. For example, I found that the Muslims like you to say, when you greet the other members, *"A salaam aleichem"* —"How's my brother?" Now that was learning a way of greeting someone. And they like you to say "All praise is due to Allah." I didn't see any reason to object to doing that, because I was primarily concerned with having this type of unity with my brothers.

I used to be very ashamed to stand up in the prison yard and pray with the Muslims. There were all these cats there who had known me all my life, cats who had been on the outside of prison with me, selling marijuana, smoking marijuana, running around doing all kinds of things, robbing everything. It was quite a change for them to see me standing up praying. I was embarrassed by that, so at first, when it was time for prayer, when the Muslims would go to pray, I would find some excuse for leaving. But then they began to look at me, and I felt guilty about that. This was a lack of solidarity, and it was embarrassing, because the other Muslims didn't approve of it. So one day I found myself down there with them with my hands outstretched praying. And after that, I prayed, you know?

I used to feel uptight sometimes when we'd go to solitary confinement. There were some fellows who really believed in God. And we would be in solitary confinement, and the prison official would be extremely angry at us, and they would feel very secure because they felt they had the protection of Allah, you know. And I would feel fucked up, because I knew that I was going to go all the way with this no matter what happened, except I didn't feel that *I* had the protection of Allah.

LOCKWOOD. Isn't it also true that the Muslims, especially Malcolm X, made an important contribution to the Black Panther ideology?

CLEAVER. There is no question about that. We try to point out specifically that we view the development of the Black Panther Party as stemming directly from what Malcolm X was teaching. Malcolm X advocated that black people arm themselves in a political fashion in order to protect themselves when they move for their rights. Malcolm made the shift of emphasis from civil rights to human rights, and he put the great emphasis on the need for black people to arm themselves so that they could defend themselves against the attacks that were being made at that time. When Malcolm X was murdered, Huey Newton and Bobby Seale saw themselves as trying to salvage the effort that was being made by Malcolm and to perpetuate it. And we in prison, we had the same reaction, because we were also very much hung up on Malcolm.

LOCKWOOD. You hadn't yet met Huey Newton when Malcolm was killed?

CLEAVER. No, we hadn't met. It's very interesting how things develop; I know now that the same thing happened outside prison that happened inside. When Malcolm X was assassinated, what he had been saying took on a new and urgent reality to the people who had been listening. While he was alive and repeating it, people were hearing it again and again, you see. But he stilled that with his blood. So it became sacred in a sense, it became very important to people. Now there was no more repetition of that, and like, that was where he took his stand. So that's what you had to deal with: how did you relate to Malcolm X, and how did you relate to his blood? And we took it up from there.

LOCKWOOD. Malcolm X had lived a desperate kind of life and then rehabilitated himself. Did you and your friends identify with him for that reason?

CLEAVER. Yes, there is a great deal of truth in it when we say "Brother Malcolm." Black convicts identify so closely with Malcolm because he represents a symbol of transformation. Here was a person who had been in the position that we were in and who had salvaged himself and gone on to make a positive contribution to the world. So we were able to gain great hope from his life, and he was a shining example to us.

LOCKWOOD. What led you from being a follower of Malcolm X to becoming a socialist revolutionary?

CLEAVER. After reading a lot of Marxist literature about their analysis of the economic system, capitalism, that we were dealing with, it seemed to me that there was no other relevant analysis that I had run across. I used to read everything from Adam Smith's *Wealth of Nations* to Karl Marx, because I was really trying to find out what it was all about. And it seemed to me that what Marx had to say about economics and political economy and all of that was most relevant, and that even if you went somewhere else, you had to start there if you wanted to understand what was going on. I've never been a member of the Communist Party. It really never attracted me because of Richard Wright. I was very much influenced by Richard Wright resigning from the Communist Party. But I consider Marxism-Leninism to be something that was not necessarily the same thing as what the Communist Party had made it. So I could feel in my gut reactions that Marxism-Leninism has something to offer and to identify with, and I could say, "Well, yes, this is the best of the truth that we have on the subject." It may really even be unnecessary to say that I'm a socialist, you see. But people who accept certain basic principles have come to be identified as socialists. I share these basic principles, and I don't have any qualms about being identified as socialist. Since it seems to be necessary to pigeonhole people, I prefer being in that pigeonhole than to any other that I know about.

LOCKWOOD. Who are the revolutionaries who have influenced you most?

CLEAVER. It would be fair to say that I am influenced by the entire revolutionary tradition. I study this tradition, because there *is* such a thing as a professional revolutionary, you know? So I've read as widely as I possibly could, and I've studied all the examples that seem to be relevant. But I guess you're asking who are my heroes? We could start ticking them off, but the list begins to get very long, because we're living in a revolutionary epoch.

LOCKWOOD. Well, who are the ones whom you relate to most personally?

CLEAVER. Obviously, the ones who were closest to my own situation. Of the black revolutionaries out of Babylon, they would be Malcolm X and Huey P. Newton and Robert Williams—people of this sort—or Bobby Seale, or Bunchy Carter. But I would say that the two individuals whom I admire above all others would be Malcolm X and Huey P. Newton.

Leaving the United States, we would have to move to Cuba and talk about Fidel Castro and Che Guevara. Leaving Cuba, we could go around the world and talk about Karl Marx, Lenin, Mao Tse-tung, Ho Chi Minh. Where do you stop? There was a time when Jomo Kenyatta was one of my heroes.

LOCKWOOD. But not any more?

CLEAVER. Well, there are problems there. I revere Jomo Kenyatta in the era of the Mau Mau.

There are many freedom fighters in the world, many of whom have given their lives for the peoples' cause. Really, going beyond symbolism and heroes, I admire and identify with everyone who stands up for the rights of the people, whether he becomes the head of a government after a revolution or whether he is shot down in an alley somewhere, an unsung hero of the revolution. I think that all the revolutionaries of the world are brothers and that they are all worthy of respect. And I respect them. I respect everybody who stands up to the forces of tyranny and oppression and says "Fuck you, I'm not going for it."

LOCKWOOD. You have written that Frantz Fanon is one of your ideological heroes. What is there in Fanon's thinking that you feel is particularly applicable to the situation of the blacks in the United States?

CLEAVER. The most important thing is that he describes the consciousness and the situation of a colonized people. Frantz Fanon was a psychiatrist, so that he was able to unravel what goes on in the mind of a colonized people. The oppressor issues propaganda to them that tries to trick them away from their revolutionary impulses, tries to make them believe that there is something wrong with being revolutionary. Take the subject of violence, for instance. A very important aspect of the process of liberation is the necessity of resorting to revolutionary violence in order to get the oppressor's boot off your neck. Fanon provides a great service to revolutionaries by explaining and analyzing the consciousness of a colonized people and showing how they move from an awareness of being oppressed all the way to the ultimate, the heighth of consciousness: the point where they're willing to fight for their freedom. He legitimizes these feelings and strips away the feelings of guilt that one might have had over, for instance, wanting to kill his slave master.

When a man is confronted by a slave master who is brutalizing him and misusing him and oppressing him and exploiting him, he wants to be free of this slave master. But the slave master refuses to let him go free, and the only way he can go free is to *break* free. Yet he has been instilled with some propaganda that stays his hand, that makes him feel guilty about reaching out with his fist and smashing his slave master in the face. When he feels guilty about that, it means that he has a hangup that in effect keeps him enslaved. Fanon explains to this man that there's nothing wrong with the way that he feels, that it's perfectly natural for him to want to hit this man, because this man in effect is hitting him in order to keep him in that position. Fanon explains and analyzes this in a way that makes it crystal-clear. And this is very important in Babylon, particularly to black people, but really to all oppressed people, because they read this and then they understand how they feel. They know what they're about, they know what they're doing, and then they move with a little more enthusiasm in the task that's before them.

LOCKWOOD. Why is Che Guevara one of your heroes? What about him do you especially admire?

CLEAVER. I don't know if I've read everything that Che Guevara has written, but I've read his *Episodes of the Revolutionary War,* I've read his *Bolivian Diary,* I've read *Socialism and Man,* and I've read his work on guerrilla warfare. I enjoyed all of those and I learned from them all. One of the most important principles that Che Guevara has to offer is his internationalist spirit. Also his fighting spirit, his ability to continue the struggle under the most awesome odds, his revolutionary courage, and his audacity. The man is like a model revolutionary. There's a quotation that I once heard in which he said that we must hate our enemy with revolutionary love. I think he had that spirit. The way that he was able to relate to the people, and his willingness to lay his life on the line repeatedly. And his unwillingness to sit behind a desk, but his need to go out and continue the struggle. I have always liked to quote when he says: "Wherever death may surprise us, let it be welcome, provided that this, our battle cry, reaches some receptive ear, and that another hand reaches out to pick up our weapons and other fighting men come forward to intone our funeral to the staccato of machine guns and new cries of battle and victory." That particular quotation is my Che Guevara.

LOCKWOOD. Are there any lessons in Che Guevara's death for you? I don't mean the fact that he is dead, but rather the fact that it was possible for his enemies to kill him and to destroy his movement—at least temporarily. Is it possible, for example, that the Black Panther Party could be destroyed if its enemies find it important enough to do so?

CLEAVER. It's quite possible to destroy any organization, you know? The point is not that Che Guevara was killed.

Many of his troops were killed, but they were not all killed, and those who survive carry on the struggle. What you learn is that the revolution did not end with Che's death. I think this would be the most insulting thing, the most bitter thing to Che Guevara, if people turned against the revolution because he was killed. I think that his life and his death were both proof against giving up the struggle. No, I don't think that that's the type of lesson that a revolutionary would draw from his defeat. You can learn many things from reading his diary. You can learn about backsliding people who don't support the struggle, and how if they had supported the struggle, maybe he would have made it. What the man was doing was a very great and epic thing, and I think it will be done someday by the successors of Che.

I'll tell you the most important thing, at least the thing that sticks in my mind most when reading Che Guevara or thinking about him. Perhaps it didn't even come from his diary or from his Bolivian experience, but maybe it's from his *Episodes of the Revolutionary War:* it is the wisdom, when laying an ambush, of shooting the first man, and the position this places the second man in. This is something very important.

LOCKWOOD. Why?

CLEAVER. He was talking about how to lay an effective ambush and how to intimidate the Army and deal with the soldiers, and the way that the military functions—you know, how they send out their scouting teams. He was talking about the importance of shooting that first man, so that when the sergeants and the lieutenants and the generals order another reconnaissance, then problems develop about who's going to be the first man out. It's not so much the killing of the first man; the point is that it makes the other soldiers think about what is their relationship to the war, and who is it that has the right to send them out there to give up their lives, and for what?

I think this is part of the guerrilla's bag, and to me, it is very important, because it poses the whole contradiction between those who are fighting for liberation and those who are fighting to implement oppression. I mean, that's where it is—the guerrilla fighter and the first man out there, and what is he doing out there?

LOCKWOOD. Do you think that handbooks and writings by other revolutionaries such as Che Guevara have specific tactical applications for the kind of guerrilla war that you expect to be fighting in the United States?

CLEAVER. There's no question about it. There are many of these military works, including the one by Mao Tsetung, and another very important book by Kwame Nkrumah, a handbook of revolutionary war. But all of these works were written for specific situations. I think that we need a handbook. As a matter of fact I *know* we need one, and I know a lot of what needs to go into it. We need a handbook for guerrilla warfare in Babylon. And somebody's going to write it.

LOCKWOOD. These books are usually written during or after a war, not before it.

CLEAVER. Well, after the war, the people who took part in it have a chance to lie back and contemplate; really what it represents is like a rehashing of the orders that were being sent out to the troops.

LOCKWOOD. But doesn't this also indicate that the tactics vary considerably according to the objective situations, and that each individual theory of guerrilla warfare has to be evolved out of the struggle itself? You yourself said that you expect to encounter quite different circumstances in the urban centers of the United States.

CLEAVER. Yes, but there's a starting point. I mean, there are certain things about the United States that we know right now which need to be disseminated to the people who will be participating in the revolutionary struggle. Simple little things like the fact that all the lights should be broken out in Babylon. This will be very important in a military situation. If people want to make a contribution to the American revolution, this is something that women, men and children, anybody can do: get a slingshot or a bee-bee gun, and go out once a night and break a light bulb or a street light and plunge the city into darkness, so the fighters can move about with a little more security. That's a small thing, but it's very important. There is really nothing the pigs can do about it except replace the light bulbs, and that becomes a task, you know?

I've talked to many people who have actually taken part in fighting in various parts of the world who seem to have the idea that America is an awesome, formidable enemy. To them it's "fortress America." But I look upon America as being a skeleton in armor. For many of us, it's as if we have lived within the belly of the monster. We know the monster and know the monster's weaknesses. For instance, there are many people around the world who are afraid of the American armed forces. But those of us who live within the United States know that essentially the American armed forces would be a very weak force when turned upon the American people. Look at the experience of the Army in Vietnam. At this moment the stockades in Babylon are full of soldiers who refuse to fight, and not just because they're cowards, but because they gained some understanding of the inhumanity of the war that's being waged in Vietnam. These stockades are full, and these men have been given large prison sentences, and they now hate the Army and they understand the Army—they understand what it is that is doing this to them. So these men are going to be some of the very valuable guerrilla fighters in the American revolution. And this is very important, because I believe that the Army is going to disintegrate rapidly and will be fighting amongst itself very soon after the revolutionary struggle is unleashed in all its fury. I believe that, and much of what I intend to do is based upon that, and there is nothing they can do about it, even though they know it in advance.

LOCKWOOD. Are you planning to proselytize in the Armed Forces?

CLEAVER. You don't have to. You proselytize by example. I think that when the generals give orders to the soldiers to go out and kill other Americans there will be a lot of soldiers who are going to stop and, instead of shooting other Americans, they're going to shoot the traitors who have given them these orders.

LOCKWOOD. You also mentioned Fidel Castro. What about him do you particularly admire?

CLEAVER. When I first heard about Fidel Castro I was in prison. I keep going back to prison. But anyway, I read his book *History Will Absolve Me* while I was in prison. This was the testimony that Fidel gave after his attack on Moncada—and having testified in court myself, you know, I marvel at him, because here was a man who literally had placed his life on the line for the welfare of his people. I admire this man's courage and selflessness and audacity, not only in attacking the Moncada, but to suffer that imprisonment, to maintain his principles and, after somehow being released from prison, to go into exile and not give up the struggle, but to return, you see, to carry on the struggle to victory, not giving a damn whether he lived or died, but fighting and carrying the struggle all the way through to the end. I mean, I related to that. I thought that was very beautiful, and I could talk about that for days.

LOCKWOOD. Perhaps your tendency to keep returning to your prison experience is significant. Many revolutionaries served time in jail. You mentioned Malcolm X and Fidel Castro; and we could add Mahatma Gandhi, Ho Chi Minh and others. Is it possible that a stretch in the brig is part of the neccessary education of a revolutionary?

CLEAVER. I think there's no doubt about it. Someone really needs to elucidate that. I think one continues to go back to prison until he gets his shit together, and then he refuses to go back, you know, and that's something else.

LOCKWOOD. You have mentioned Huey Newton several times. Why do you consider him one of your two most important revolutionary heroes?

CLEAVER. I hope I can capture some part of that. I have spent a great deal of time thinking about Huey. In trying to express what I see to be the essential quality in Huey, the thing that is like a key to his character, I called it "the courage to kill." By that I meant not the courage that we usually talk about when we recognize that people have done something worthy of being commended, but a very exceptional quality related to a man who is in misery, a man who is suffering because of the condition of his people, a man who is unable to be comfortable, unable to adjust to the oppression that his people are subjected to, a man who is forced, who has no choice, because of some inner quality. . . .

I used to say that Huey is some type of mutation. I've never known anyone like Huey. I've known all kinds of people, you know. I've known soldiers who have gone to war; I've known robbers who have placed their lives on the line to commit robberies; I've known people who have risked their lives to protect someone; I've known people who were subsequently killed in political activities and also in crimes. I've known people who were tough guys, who didn't give a damn about dying, didn't care whether they lived or died. But that doesn't relate to Huey, because Huey loves life.

To my surprise, I found that Huey plays the piano. He went to some type of conservatory, and he plays concert piano. I remember one time we had had a violent encounter with a rival political organization in San Francisco. Afterwards, we were all in this house. There had been some shooting, and we thought perhaps someone was dead. It turned out that there was no one injured or shot, and nothing came of it. But during the period when we did not know what had happened, there was a piano in this house, and Huey sat down and started playing it, and there was concert music. Well, there was like a wistful look in his eyes that I had never seen before. It reminded me of another time when there was a disciplinary problem within the ranks, and Huey asked if there was anyone else who wanted to be the Minister of Defense. He said he'd rather not have that position, because it was a burden, and if anyone else wanted it, to please take it. He wasn't lying. He really meant that. Because Huey knew, you see, that he might be killed at any time. He knew that, and he was very serious about that, and he had accepted it, and it just added to his burden to have people adding to the risk involved.

I'm trying to remember the expressions that I've seen on his face when I've seen him in uptight situations. It seems to me that he is at his best when he is in the position of standing as a shield between his people and the oppressors, particularly policemen, and particularly when they're armed. In that kind of a situation Huey transcends himself. He speaks the pure truth, and he relates to the justice of the situation and what the rights involved are. There is no frivolous conversation, and what he says is pure and simple, and I've seen the strange effect that this has on the cops. They cannot deal with that. I've seen Huey face cops down by just running down the situation, and the justice of it, and the fact that there is a violation of human rights involved.

Well, I still don't feel that I've said what I really want to say: that when a man accepts a certain role or position, and he's fulfilling that position, it seems that he is kind of transformed. I see Huey as a person who was transformed, a person who had, by placing his life on the line, gained another form of life, or more life. Huey was totally alive, and every moment was important. He filled every moment with something. I think that Huey is a historic figure, a pivotal figure. I think that in terms of historical continuity, among the major figures who have carried the football further down the field, you will move from Malcolm X to Stokely Carmichael, and almost simultaneously you will encounter Huey Newton. But there's a short span between Malcolm X and Stokely Carmichael, and I think that as our historical perspective becomes clear, we will recognize more of a continuity between Malcolm X and Huey Newton. Huey's message is just beginning to get across, just beginning to transform people, and people will write history with the coming of Huey Newton.

LOCKWOOD. What is Huey Newton's message?

CLEAVER. Essentially what's very important about Huey is that he destroyed the whole abstract discussion about the way that black people should move for their liberation. Many people talked about placing the struggle of black people on the same basis of reality that the liberation struggles all over the world inevitably reach, but it was Huey who organized this idea and created an instrument, a political party that would be the vehicle for galvanizing this idea into reality by making black males into men, by setting the standard of what a black man must be and must be willing to do in our time in order to be a man and in order to say that he is fulfilling his duties to secure his tribe. I think Huey has set a standard against which other men will be measured.

LOCKWOOD. Because he was the one who saw the need to establish a party?

CLEAVER. Not just the Party, you see, but a fighting party that is willing to stand up and not only be willing to die. Huey showed that you also have to have that other degree, what I called "the courage to kill": the courage not only to risk your life, but to take the initiative in the pursuit of your liberation and your freedom and be willing to take the life of your oppressor when he's moving to take your life. People in an oppressed position don't have to wait for their oppressor to make an overt act of aggression against them personally. For he has already aggressed upon your people at the moment that he put you in the position of oppression, you see? So, the point is, to move, to get the boot off your neck, to reach up at that boot and to grapple with it.

LOCKWOOD. You mentioned Stokely Carmichael. At one time not long ago, Stokely Carmichael was the principal spokesman for black power in the United States. Recently, though, we've heard very little about him. After he left SNCC and became Prime Minister of the Black Panther Party he seems to have disappeared from public view. Do you know why?

CLEAVER. We in the Black Panther Party have been very disappointed with Stokely. After the OLAS meeting at Havana in 1967, he traveled around and visited many of the revolutionary capitols of the world, and when he returned, he made his first public speech on Huey P. Newton's birthday, February seventeenth, at the Oakland Auditorium, in Oakland, California. This was a major rally that turned out thousands of people, and it was held on the eve of Huey's trial. At that rally, we appointed Stokely Prime Minister of the Black Panther Party because we felt that he had distinguished himself above everyone else who was a possible candidate for that position.

But Stokely did not satisfy the duties that were placed upon him. He did not fulfill his responsibilities in terms of relating to organizational structure and of moving in an organized fashion. It was not a question of discipline, because there was no one trying to impose discipline on him; rather, it was a question of his going in a lone-wolf fashion, of not permitting us to coordinate activity with him, of not staying in touch with the organization, things of this type. I don't want to go into any more detail than that, except to say, in response to your question, that we really don't know what Stokely is doing. We do know that he is not fulfilling his duties as Prime Minister of the Black Panther Party, and to that extent we are disappointed.

LOCKWOOD. What do you think went wrong?

CLEAVER. I don't know. I spent much time with Brother Stokely. I traveled with him when he was at the peak of his sojourn, while he was articulating his concepts of black power. I traveled throughout the South with him and throughout the North; I heard him speak on many occasions to jam-packed houses; I saw him give new life and new hope to black people; I saw him electrify audiences with his articulation; I saw him teach; I saw him make people better qualified to live and also to struggle. I mean, I saw Stokely doing something great, and I had great admiration for Stokely, and I still—I *dig* Stokely Carmichael, you know? But I'm pissed off at him. And I will not say that there's anything final about it. I mean, Stokely might be putting some shit together that would deal with the situation and rescue everybody, I don't know.

LOCKWOOD. Have you been in touch with him?

CLEAVER. I have not been in touch with him recently, no. That's one of the problems, you see, that we're not in touch with him, and he knows we want to get in touch with him, and he doesn't respond. He might be dead for all I know.

LOCKWOOD. After you came out of jail and went to work for *Ramparts* magazine, wasn't one of your first assignments to follow Stokely and write about him? Wasn't your article called "My Father and Stokely Carmichael"?

CLEAVER. Yes, that was somebody's idea. Stokely said, when he saw it, "My father, comma, Stokely Carmichael."

LOCKWOOD. *Ramparts* is a predominantly white-staffed magazine. Although it's a leftist magazine, it is in a sense a part of the mass media and therefore part of what you identify as the power structure. Have you ever felt any contradiction about your role there?

CLEAVER. No, I never did feel any conflict there. I became aware of *Ramparts* while I was in prison. In the prisons of the state of California *Ramparts* is contraband. I used to get hold of it through devious means. And I, along with many other convicts, dug *Ramparts* magazine. So I was very delighted when I had an opportunity to go to work for *Ramparts* when I got out, and I found that generally, throughout the movement, both in the black section of the struggle and in the white section of the struggle, it had a very acceptable reputation and could gain access where other magazines could not enter. *Ramparts* takes a position on issues, and I would classify it as an underground magazine. I would say that it is not part of the power structure just because it is part of the mass media. We have a newspaper in the Black Panther Party, and I don't consider that to be a part of the establishment media.

I used to think of *Ramparts* as being the Ministry of Information of the American revolution, because it was dealing with the struggle both in the white community and in the black community. I felt it was performing a valuable service, so I never felt uptight about my relationship to it. There were people who *did* feel uptight about that. There were people who felt that this was contradictory. They felt that *Ramparts* was a white magazine, you see. But I don't know; I think that if I had stayed in Babylon I might have become the editor-in-chief.

LOCKWOOD. Would you still like to be editor-in-chief of *Ramparts?*

CLEAVER. [Laughing] *Yes.* I had a program for *Ramparts,* you know.

LOCKWOOD. What was that?

CLEAVER. Well . . . I think I'd better save it and see if I can become the editor-in-chief.

LOCKWOOD. Besides being an editor of *Ramparts,* you have given interviews to a lot of the white press—

CLEAVER. Why do you call it "the white press"? That's an un-American term. That's an un-American concept.

LOCKWOOD. Well, I'm trying to put myself in your place. I'm trying to express what I thought was your way of looking at it. You correct me if I'm wrong.

CLEAVER. What do you work for, *Ebony* magazine? That's part of the white press? Well, I know what you're talking about, but I—you know, just saying that says something about America that's very important. Because I believe that *black* people in the United States are oppressed and that *white* people in the United States are oppressed. I don't believe that there's one ruling class oppressing black people and another ruling class oppressing white people. It's very clear that there's one class oppressing both black people and white people and Mexican people, Puerto Rican people, all the people. It's just that they use racism as a policy in their oppression of black people, and they use class as their instrument in their oppression of white people. But it's really one ruling class with a policy towards all the various groups that make up the United States. So that I don't call it the white press; I call it the pig press, because you have to make a distinction between the people and the pigs.

LOCKWOOD. But there are, you will admit, some black militants who do talk about "the white press" and say Don't talk to the "white devils," don't work with them, etc. Yet the Black Panther Party seems to be moving closer to a political coalition with white activist groups.

CLEAVER. This is true. It comes out of the political analysis which we have made of our situation in the United States. We feel that there's the mother country in America and that there's also the black colony—that the black people represent a colonized people, a domestic colony. And we say that what is needed in the United States is liberation in the colony and revolution in the mother country, because oppression of the black people in the United States is a national question, and oppression of the white people is a class question. Now, there are grievances that are specific to the colony, but there are other grievances that are general to both the mother country and to the colony. And as we tear down the walls of the colony, as we destroy what we call "community imperialism," whereby the black community is subjected to the manipulation and control of the white community—as we destroy these specific obstacles, we feel that what will then become most important will be the general grievances that are shared by all of the oppressed peoples in America. And I think we are reaching that point; we're reaching the point where the struggle has to be a united-front struggle, and where machinery has to be created that will reach across the boundary between the mother country and the colony. We need machinery in America that can move in two directions at the same time. What we need is a coalition between the forces in the black community which are working on the national question and the forces in the white community which are working on the class question, whereby they can make a common thrust against their common oppressor.

LOCKWOOD. How will this coalition be made up? Which are the elements among the black militants and which are the elements among white militants who would form such a coalition?

CLEAVER. I'm through with militants. I'm through with black militants and I'm through with white militants. I'm not interested in any coalitions between militants. As far as I'm concerned, the militants can join the Republican Party. I'm interested in coalitions between white revolutionaries, black revolutionaries, Mexican-American revolutionaries, Chinese revolutionaries, Chinese-American revolutionaries—let me stipulate that—Puerto Rican revolutionaries, all down the line.

LOCKWOOD. But which organized groups, then?

CLEAVER. I want to move away from groups. But we could talk about SDS. I think that there are beautiful people there. We could talk about the Young Lords, which is a Puerto Rican group. We could talk about the Young Patriots, which is a group of young whites. We could talk about the Brown Berets, which is a group of young Mexican-Americans. We could talk about the Red Guard, which is a group of young Chinese-Americans. Those are just some of the groups that I know about. I know their names, but it's not so much the name of the group that's important, it's the activity that these people are involved in. What we need in the United States is a North American Liberation Front that would not be either a black or a white organization, a Mexican organization or a Puerto Rican or any other. It would just be a machinery that would unite the revolutionary forces in all of the communities so that they could carry out their activity in a coordinated and disciplined manner. People who are revolutionaries transcend all of these community boundaries and relate to humanity in general.

LOCKWOOD. You said before that you consider the Black Panther Party to be the vanguard of the black revolution.

Are there any other black organizations which you also consider to be in the vanguard and which might participate in such a coalition?

CLEAVER. There are a lot of groups and organizations that are doing meaningful work. I'm very interested in and I have a lot of respect for a group called the Republic of New Africa. But I'm not sure that I would put any other organization in the black community on the level of the Black Panther Party. I don't like to go around and proclaim that the Black Panther Party is the vanguard. I think that one proves one's role by one's activity. But it seems crystal-clear to me that the Black Panther Party has catapulted far beyond the level reached by any other organization so far.

Now, we talk about the vanguard for a specific reason. We feel that, in terms of revolutionary theory, the most oppressed people in a given social entity are likely to be the most revolutionary people. There are likely to be more grievances in the area that is most oppressed. This means that there are more people who are uptight in that area, therefore more urgency for solutions and a greater likelihood that revolutionaries and revolutionary ideology will be produced in that area. We say that black people are the most oppressed people in America, and for that reason they have more motivation to move than others. But I'm not saying that other people are not oppressed. Really, the most oppressed man in America is the American Indian. But because there are more blacks in America than there are Indians, there seems to be more happening in the black areas. Maybe the day will come when the Indian will be the vanguard of the revolution. I would welcome that day, because I would like to stand right behind Huey Newton with Huey standing right behind a reincarnation of Sitting Bull.

LOCKWOOD. What are your opinions on the "black cultural nationalism" movement, which seems to be growing in popularity in the United States, especially on the campuses, and which seems to contradict some of the principles which you have stated? Recently, Harold Cruse, one of the leading proponents of black cultural nationalism, writing in *The New York Review of Books,* strongly criticized what he views as your excessive emphasis on violence and armed struggle as the means of attaining the goals which he posits as being common to all American blacks. Cruse says that there is "another" revolution going on in the United States on behalf of the blacks. He calls it a "cultural revolution." He says: "Thus in the midst of our racial and social crisis [he means that of the entire country] does a 'cultural revolution' begin to gather momentum. The crisis of education is a cultural crisis, with the students' unrest as its natural corollary. Decentralization of ghetto schools, the drive for black studies in the colleges and in the universities become the main expression of black cultural nationalism. But in his dismissal of cultural nationalism, Eldridge Cleaver completely misses the real meaning of all this."

CLEAVER. I consider Harold Cruse to be an ideologist for the black bourgeoisie. He makes a great point of all this stuff that's happened on the campuses. He defends this as being "cultural nationalism." But if you just stop and think a minute you'll realize who in the black community is able to send his children to college? He is not what Malcolm X called the "field nigger," not what we of the Black Panther Party call "the brothers and the sisters off the block," which means the same thing. That is, the man in the ghetto by and large is not even able to get his child all the way through high school, let alone to college. Those who make it to the colleges are the children of the black middle class. And it's very significant that the blacks who are most into cultural nationalism are the children of the middle class. For instance, we could talk about the man who created the Black Students Union at San Francisco State College, Jimmy Garrity. And we could talk about Ron Karenga and LeRoi Jones.

LOCKWOOD. What do you think of Ron Karenga?

CLEAVER. I'm going to tell you . . . Both LeRoi Jones and Ron Karenga are products of the middle class, the black middle class. They're both men who went to college, and they are both chief spokesmen for what is called cultural nationalism. Now I'm not saying that cultural nationalism in and of itself *was* a bad thing. I'm saying that there is a dialectical relationship involved, that at one time it was progressive but that now it has become reactionary. And I think that this is because the black middle class is the element that is most alienated from its roots. If you read E. Franklin Fraser's book *The Black Bourgeoisie* you can get some insight into this. These are the people who were surprised to find out that they were black.

LOCKWOOD. What do you mean, they were surprised to find out they were black?

CLEAVER. Because this element had gone as far as any element in the black community has ever been allowed to do towards being assimilated into white society. They had learned to talk like white people, walk like white people, dress like white people, think like white people. What we refer to as having a black body and a white mind. They adopted all of the standards of white middle-class society, and they sought to enter the mainstream of America, you see? But then they found that they were being rebuffed by their black skin or by the texture of their hair. The things that were holding them back were the things that they hated and that they had suppressed. They wanted to transcend their blackness and be white. So when the change came down, this was the element that was most uptight in terms of regaining its roots, because they had farther to move along the scale to get back home, you see.

People say that the Black Muslims represent the very lowest levels in the black community. And this is very true, but there's a very great distinction between what we call the cultural nationalists and the Black Muslims. All black people went through a cultural nationalist phase,

more or less starting in 1956, when Ghana became an independent country, when the bus boycott started in Montgomery, Alabama, and when the Black Muslims were beginning to be known, not so much throughout the United
States, but in the black communities. There was something like an awakening to a new identity, in which black
people discovered that their hair was beautiful, that their
black skin was beautiful and that they had a history and
an ancestral homeland. You know: "Black is beautiful!"
"I'm black and I'm proud!" and all of that. This was a
phenomenon that took place at that initial awakening.
When this took place, the black bourgeoisie was the last
to respond; but when it did respond it turned it into a
fetish, into some kind of freak dance. It misunderstood
totally what was going on and turned it into a cult, while
other people continued to move, like Stokely, who used to
say, "Blackness is necessary, but it's not sufficient." I
mean, after you find out that you're still black, that
doesn't mean that you're going to be free, but you must
continue to fight on as a black man. This is in contrast to
cultural nationalism, people who stop there, thinking that
once you learn how to speak Swahili or wear African
clothes or let your hair go long and grow out a natural
or an "Afro," that you're free. There are some organizations that teach that. Ron Karenga teaches that you can't
begin to become free until you learn how to speak Swahili,
until you do all these things. This is cultural nationalism,
but Malcolm X opened up the door to revolutionary black
nationalism.

LOCKWOOD. You spoke about the bus boycott in Montgomery, which was the beginning of Dr. Martin Luther King's rise to importance in the black movement. Where would you place King's movement and his doctrine of nonviolence in the history of the black struggle in the United States?

CLEAVER. I think that Martin Luther King was a very important man both to black people and to white people. I think that the man exhausted a myth, one that he was greatly responsible not for creating but for formulating. The idea of black people being nonviolent and passive, of course, goes back to the plantation, where, when the slave master disciplined you and beat you with a whip, you were not expected to strike back.

You could say that Martin Luther King was telling white America to put its money where its mouth is. He took this tradition of passiveness that started on the plantation and he said, "Here we are. We want our freedom. We are going to have our freedom. But in the interests of peace, in the interests of avoiding a holocaust, let's realize that black people are serious and that they're not going to accept anything short of their full freedom. Be reasonable, and realize that it would be best for all if we did this peacefully. We have suffered so long, and we are still suffering, but here we are, and we're still nonviolent, so what are you going to do, white man?" And so they killed him, you see? So black people look at that and say, "Well we can do no more in that direction.

That policy has failed. It doesn't work not to hit the slave master back when he beats you with the whip, and these other men have been saying that we should get a whip and strike the slave master back. We've tried not striking back; that didn't work, so let's try striking back." Even while Martin Luther King was alive, many people in the black community were incensed at him because they were convinced—and I was among them—that non-violence was not going to work. I remember what Malcolm X said about that. He said that anyone who teaches us to be nonviolent towards the white man, instead of teaching us to get away from the white man while he continues to be brutal towards us, is a traitor to his people.

I think that Martin Luther King performed a disservice to his people by carrying his policy of nonviolence to absurd lengths. But the man was dedicated to that policy, so he was going to live and die on that. But it would have been very welcome to me, if, after all of his confrontations with white racism and the power structure, Martin Luther King had said, "Okay, brothers and sisters—I was wrong. I have failed, so now I advise you to lay down the Bible and pick up the gun." But then again—and I have to say all of this because I'm somewhat ambivalent about Martin Luther King—it may ultimately be that Martin Luther King had some impact on America in its guts somewhere, and that it will be because of the lengths to which he went that we can be successful in our revolutionary struggle.

LOCKWOOD. You mean that he may have helped to prepare the way?

CLEAVER. He may have. He may have added something to some balance we don't know about. Certainly, what the man was doing was not insignificant. He was having an effect on people, and in the long run it's the cumulative effect that's important. But while I would never say that I'm glad that he's dead, I would say that I am glad that black people are no longer practicing nonviolence.

LOCKWOOD. He certainly dramatized his cause. He gave blacks a certain consciousness that they didn't have before, and I think it's clear that he also affected the consciousness of white America in terms of its understanding of the black struggle.

CLEAVER. Well, I don't know. What you say may be true, I don't know. But yes, Martin Luther King touched people deeply. He stirred people deeply. He got down in the soul. He got hold of whatever morality was left in the American soul, you know? He was like a man scratching through the dump or through garbage cans looking for a pearl. And I don't know if he found it or not, but I know that when the assassin's bullet struck him down, he was still scratching, you dig?

LOCKWOOD. As an individual and as a Black Panther, you are committed to a violent revolutionary struggle to overthrow the American government. Why, then, did you run as a candidate for President in the Peace and Freedom Party in the 1968 election?

CLEAVER. I'd like to begin by saying that I am committed to meeting the violence of the oppressor with the violence of the oppressed, meeting counter-revolutionary violence with revolutionary violence. I decided to run, if you want to call it that, on the Peace and Freedom Party ticket, but I would not say that I was running for President. I was running for the revolutionary movement. Since the American people are in the habit of focusing their attention on the issues during the presidential election, it seemed to me to offer a forum for articulating our views. There was an opportunity to reach a lot of people, so I took that opportunity to articulate what we were trying to get across to the American people. And, as I have said before, if through some quirk of circumstances I would have been elected President, I would not have entered the White House, but I would have burned it down and turned it into a museum or a monument to the decadence of the past.

I feel that the electoral process is most unviable, you see, particularly in the rigged political machinery that we have in the United States of America. Certainly, I had no illusions about going into the political arena and having what I was saying acted upon. I was not talking to the pigs or the power structure—though I cursed at them now and then. I was talking to the people, talking *with* the people, I would prefer to say. And another of the main considerations that I had in mind was that I believed that 1968 was the last presidential campaign that would be conducted under capitalism in the United States. I believe that by 1972 we will have a military *coup* in the United States and a military dictatorship, because by that time there will be a full-scale war going on in the United States, and an election for the presidency will be out of the question. The pigs of the power structure will find it out of the question, and the revolutionaries will find it out of the question. That was the last campaign, as far as I was concerned, so there was no particular danger of setting a negative example or of making people think that electoral politics were relevant.

LOCKWOOD. Well, 1972 is less than three years away, Eldridge. What are the signs that you see from your vantage point here in exile that indicate that there will be a military *coup* in the United States by 1972?

CLEAVER. I see the same things going on in America that everybody else sees. It's just that I interpret what's happening there in this particular way.

LOCKWOOD. But what are the signs? Can you go into detail?

CLEAVER. I see that the last straw has already been placed on the camel's back, and the camel's back is broken, and the war is already going on.

LOCKWOOD. That's very metaphorical and rather general.

CLEAVER. Look—don't you know that there's a war going on in America? Do you think that there are just a few sporadic outbursts going on?

LOCKWOOD. I'm asking you to describe the evidence which you see that there is a war going on in the United States.

CLEAVER. I see that the enemy has been identified and that the victims of this enemy are resisting. The enemy is killing more and more victims, and the victims are killing more and more of the enemy. I'm saying that these things have a way of escalating overnight, and I'm saying that within the next three years there will be sharp escalations on both sides and that it will become clear to everybody that there's a real war going on. But if you just look at what's happening now, you can see there's a war going on.

LOCKWOOD. Do you feel that the Vietnamese war is playing a part in the radicalization of the situation?

CLEAVER. I think that the Vietnamese war has been decisive and that it will be decisive in more than one respect, because many of the revolutionaries who are going to make the revolution are in the ranks of the military, and they will be coming home. Many of them have already come back home. Many of them are in the stockades of the military throughout the United States and really throughout the world, because wherever they have a military base, they have a stockade.

LOCKWOOD. Now, a lot of radicals besides yourself talk about making the American revolution, while many others who might like to see one are skeptical that it can ever take place. It seems to me that one of the problems that those who wish to make a revolution in the United States have encountered thus far is their disability to organize themselves, to get together in coalition and take on a united program for a revolution. You have also spoken about the need for organizing a united front—but can it be done?

CLEAVER. I think that those who are professional revolutionaries, or people who are principally dedicated to the revolutionary struggle, must first of all make an accurate analysis of the situation and then adopt correct tactics based on that analysis. And then you have to start talking about ideology. And what is ideology? As far as I'm concerned, ideology is not a prayer; it's not a poem; it's not something that like you read in a book and you memorize. What it is is a definition of the situation that confronts you. Like, what Karl Marx did was to make a study of the capitalistic system and then to define how this system operated and to formulate the workings of the system into language that people could understand. He communicated with people, and they call that an ideology. But what it was was a definition of the reality that prevailed. So people need to define the situation that exists. Once we know what the analysis is, then we have to understand which tactics are indicated by this analysis, and then we have to have the courage to implement those tactics. That is clear; that is what is called for. What is not clear is: Can we do it? Can we find it in ourselves to undertake the task?

LOCKWOOD. If the analysis is clear, as you say, and the situation has been defined, why has it been so difficult for the various radical and activist groups to get together until now? For example, why can't the SDS work directly with the Black Panthers?

CLEAVER. I don't understand what you mean when you say "Why can't they?" because they do. The SDS and the Black Panther Party recognize the work that each is doing. I know that there is much factionalism in the ranks of the revolutionary movement in the United States. But this has always been true in any country that has undergone a revolutionary process. It is through the process of the revolution itself that these antagonisms are eliminated, because they are really based on disagreements over tactics and the like. But there seems to be some general agreement on the over-all situation, that this is a situation that needs to be struggled against. I think that each and every group that is in the movement wouldn't be in the movement if it didn't feel that way. It would be on the other side saying "No, this is not a situation that needs to be struggled against." So there's agreement on the major principle, but there is disagreement on how you go about dealing with it.

LOCKWOOD. What we are talking about now is the process by which people who want to make a revolution get together and mount an effort to take power. But it has often been said that the real revolution only begins *after* you have taken power.

CLEAVER. This has been said mostly by people who have waged a successful revolutionary struggle and who find themselves in power and see that they're up against the wall. They know that they lose as much sleep, work just as hard, in fact probably harder, that there's more heart-break involved than they experienced when it was just a question of the struggle. The struggle to take power is a process of destruction, and it has always been easier to destroy than it has been to build. It's much easier to put a bomb under some oppressive structure than it is to scrape up the rubble and to build—first of all to conceive the type of structure that should be erected on the ruins, and then to build that structure and also deal with the counter-revolutionary forces and other hostile elements.

LOCKWOOD. Do you have any ideas of your own about the kinds of institutions that might be created to insure the communication between the leaders and the masses, the participation of the people in their own self-government?

CLEAVER. Once the revolution is secured against all forms of counter-revolution that may be encountered, it will be necessary to establish organizations from top to bottom so that people can participate in the discussions that are going on and can have their will counted when the decisions are being made. I'm not saying that you will have bourgeois elections—that's out of the question. But I'm saying that there is another form of organizing people so that they can participate in all these discussions.

Maybe that's still abstract. Anyway, to me it's really not the pressing consideration. I only respond to that question academically, because I think that the duty at hand is to make the revolution. Those who are making the revolution should concentrate foremost on that. If they have the time to go into detail about designing the new society, they can do it, but I think the job of making the revolution is large enough that full time is required. And I have faith that there will always be people at hand who will be able to carry on the struggle at whatever level it is left off by those who preceded. If every revolutionary who participated in the revolution were suddenly to die on the day the revolution triumphed, I think that people would arise to carry it on and to establish the system that was fought for. I mean, that's the way human society moves.

LOCKWOOD. In some of your writings you have proposed a rather novel innovation in socialist ideology: the ideal of "male–female fulfillment." You have described your vision of the ideal society as "a society in which a man and a woman come as close as possible to total unity on the basis of mutual attraction." I assume that this was not a frivolous aside, but a serious belief. Would you explain what you mean by that phrase?

CLEAVER. You see, there's a crisis between men and women, particularly in Babylon. They have great difficulty in having a healthy relationship. I refer to people, man and woman, as each one of them being one half of a whole. I think that when you look at either a man or a woman, you're only looking at one half of one unit of the species, you see. Just in order to think about it, you could postulate that at some time in the history of evolution there once was a creature that was not split into halves. He was a unitary creature that combined all of the functions that are now distributed in male and female. And, in order to cope with the environment, some decision was made in that mechanism to divide. I believe that there's a powerful magnetism between the male and the female, and that this magnetism is there to ensure that these two halves that are split will always be able to reunite in order to fulfill their functions.

But the social structure can interfere. The mind can be molded in such a way that this harmonious unity can be impeded. So that in a society that's all fucked up, the relationship is going to be all fucked up. But a society that allowed people to blossom, a society that nurtured life, would also nurture the relationship between man and woman and maximize their ability to relate and to unite and to experience a moment of supreme ecstacy.

LOCKWOOD. In the revolutionary society that you envision, would part of the technology be harnessed to engineer this kind of possibility, or would it just happen spontaneously?

CLEAVER. I don't think that it has to be engineered, because I think it is something that would just happen naturally if everything else that is happening is good and working for people.

LOCKWOOD. In other words, those people who grew up deformed by the old social structure would, under the revolution, simply lose their old hangups?

CLEAVER. Well, say that, by some miracle, a hungup cat like LBJ might escape the firing squad. I know I'm stretching the imagination a little by saying that, but just say that through some miracle of mercy he was not executed. I think that you could place *him* in the geographical and spiritual center of utopia and he would still be all fucked up, you know?

LOCKWOOD. It seems to me that anybody who is committed to the idea of revolution requires an essential faith in the perfectability of man. Do you believe in the perfectability of man?

CLEAVER. Perfectability?

LOCKWOOD. That man is basically good and can eliminate from his character feelings of egotism and greed, that he can learn to substitute collectivism for individual concern, and so on. This ideal seems common to all revolutionaries.

CLEAVER. Yes, it's just that that word "perfectability" seems to be an extremist term.

LOCKWOOD. Maybe you have a better one?

CLEAVER. Well, I would just say that it is possible to create an environment in which men will relate to each other as brothers and not as enemies, where they will be able to cooperate with each other and to struggle together to improve their situation. I don't differ with you in how you define perfectability. It's just that that term is too absolute.

LOCKWOOD. Then let's not use the term. Do you believe that man is essentially good and can act for good, if shown the way?

CLEAVER. Yes, I like people, and I think that they're good. And I don't even believe that you have to show them the way. I think you just have to get out of their way, you know? It's like a flower or a bud. You don't have to teach a flower or a bud how to bloom. You just have to let it live. You don't have to teach a tree how to be a tree, you know, and I don't think you have to teach people how to be human. I think you have to teach them how to stop being *inhumane*.

LOCKWOOD. And you think that's possible?

CLEAVER. I mean I think it's easy, you know, if you can dig it.

LOCKWOOD. You are about to become a father. Are you looking forward to that? Do you have time to think about it?

CLEAVER. Well, I don't know. I mean, I'm going through changes about that, you know. I'm very delighted about it. I didn't think that I would ever—somewhere inside me, you know, I've always wanted to be a father. I want a little boy. When I say that to Kathleen, she says I'm a male chauvinist. But if it's a little girl, I can dig it. Well, you know I'll be even more responsible, because—you see children are really the people that I dig. I remember a period in my life when I was hung up on talking to children. I knew a girl once who had some little children. And I noticed that she never talked to them. She always screamed at them and she would treat them as though they were stupid. I looked at her little boy, and the cat was uptight, and he was like *enraged*. Every time I saw him he seemed to be *enraged,* and I wondered what was wrong with him, you know? I observed the situation, and it occurred to me that it was just because no one talked to him, that he was being treated as though he couldn't think or that he wasn't a sensible person, and that they seemed to be waiting for him to get older, and then he would start thinking. So I started talking to him. And it was very clear to me that you could hold an intelligent conversation with the child. I brought this to her attention and I made her start talking to the cat, you know, and he just changed, because he was being communicated with. Even though he couldn't really talk good, he could communicate.

LOCKWOOD. What kind of society do you think your child—your son or your daughter—will live in?

CLEAVER. Well, if I have anything to do about it he's going to live in utopia. I don't know what else to say.

LOCKWOOD. Eldridge Cleaver believes in utopia.

CLEAVER. Right on!

LOCKWOOD. In *Soul on Ice* you told how when you were eighteen years old you got caught with what you called "a shopping bag full of love." You were carrying some pot around. And Robert Scheer, in an article about you, offered the idea that if you hadn't become a Panther, you probably would have become a bohemian writer. Are you a bohemian? Is there that side of you?

CLEAVER. I mean, I don't know about all of these terms out of Berkeley. I mean this is a Berkeleyesque description of a man. I never called myself a bohemian.

LOCKWOOD. Is there something wrong with being a bohemian?

CLEAVER. No, it's just not a part of my vocabulary in terms of describing myself. If I were describing Bob Scheer, I might call *him* a bohemian. I don't consider myself a bohemian, but I'm not an uptight formal cat either. I'm loose. Like I don't like to wear suits, for instance. I believe in living a life that's not uptight. I mean, I just believe in being myself. Well, I don't know—fuck Eldridge Cleaver! I can't relate to describing myself. I mean, fuck that, you know. I like to get high, if that's what you mean. But I have to say that I found out that particularly those who are involved in a revolutionary struggle would do well to keep a clear head at all times, because even though a lot of the pigs get drunk, and they may be moving against you while they're drunk, if you're trying to wage the struggle, you're fighting an uphill battle and you've got to have all your wits about you. But, of course, this would relate to the discipline under which you're functioning. If you have established rules that will permit you to turn on, I would say yeah, that's okay with me. I wouldn't get uptight about that at all.

You see, I look upon this whole thing as like, the oppressor is wasting people's time. To me, that's what it simply boils down to, because there are other things that I would like to be doing. But you're being interfered with, and you know that you can't do your thing, because if you don't pay attention to what's going on around you, you may be sitting under a tree, you know, reading some poems and smoking a joint and talking to your other half, and some pigs will come by and drag you to the gas chamber or shoot you or crack your head. So you have to get up from beneath that tree, remembering that what you want to do is to get back to that tree just as soon as you possibly can, and so like, get up and sober up and come down off your trip and deal with the pig, and then you can talk about going back to do your thing.

LOCKWOOD. Obviously, you are a man who enjoys life a great deal. But you are also a man who is disciplining himself to be a revolutionary. What do you consider your biggest failings, the things about yourself that you must work hardest to overcome?

CLEAVER. Talking too much. I think that's my biggest problem. I'm a fat mouth and a fool, you know? I talk too much.